P9-AOD-537

THE **NEW VEGAN** COOKBOOK

INNOVATIVE **VEGETARIAN** RECIPES
FREE OF DAIRY, EGGS, AND **CHOLESTEROL**

BY **LORNA SASS**

PHOTOGRAPHS BY **JONELLE WEAVER**

D1174724

CHRONICLE BOOKS
SAN FRANCISCO

THIS COLLECTION OF RECIPES IS DEDICATED TO COOKS WHO AGREE THAT
"THE DISCOVERY OF A NEW DISH DOES MORE FOR THE HAPPINESS OF MANKIND
THAN THE DISCOVERY OF A STAR."

(BRILLAT-SAVARIN, 1755–1826)

This edition published in 2010 exclusively for Barnes & Noble, Inc.,
by Chronicle Books LLC.

Text copyright © 2001 by Lorna Sass.
Photographs © 2001 by Jonelle Weaver.
All rights reserved. No part of this book may be reproduced
in any form without written permission from the publisher.

Library of Congress Cataloging-in-Publication data available under
ISBN 0-8118-2760-7.

ISBN 978-1-4351-2567-4

Manufactured in China.

Design by Sara Schneider.
Food styling by Victoria Granoff and Melanie Harvin.
Prop styling by Loren Simons and Paige Hicks.
Typesetting by Jaime Robles.
Cover design by Sarah Pulver.
Tupperware is a registered trademark of Dart Industries, Inc.

The photographer wishes to thank Victoria Granoff and Melanie Harvin
for their beautiful food, Loren Simons for her gorgeous props, Paige
Hicks for her production/styling assistance, Jordan Hollender, and
Sara Schneider at Chronicle Books for the opportunity to work on
such a great project.

10 9 8 7 6 5 4 3 2 1

Chronicle Books LLC
680 Second Street
San Francisco, CA 94107
www.chroniclebooks.com

ACKNOWLEDGMENTS

Attempts to tame a dish by caging it into a recipe are always daunting because the transformation of raw into cooked rarely happens the same way twice. Nevertheless, with the help of my dear recipe-testing "elves," I have done my best to accommodate the vagaries of ingredients and taste.

First and foremost, I offer heartfelt thanks to super-elves Cathy Roberts and Marcia Kindlmann. Cathy has encouraged me with unfailing generosity through many books, kindly pointing out potential trouble spots, conversing with me through her detailed notes, and decorating the pages with a coveted star when she and Neil enjoyed their dinner. Marcia graciously transformed the solitary nature of recipe development into a collaborative effort through her discerning e-mail reflections on creativity, clarity, and preferred brands and her cheerful reports on husband Pete's response to last night's vegan dinner. I am very grateful to Tristan Roberts and Glen Kindlmann for inspiring their moms to be such dedicated vegan cooks!

Many others contributed their time and energy to this project. My devoted group of elves includes Judy Bloom, Nancy Brin, Heather and Gerhard Bock, Banoo and Jeevak Parpia, and Rosemary Serviss. Sally O'Brien helped me launch the project and, when she brought over some slow-roasted tomatoes, prompted me to keep the oven turned on. Michele Lunt assisted me during most of the recipe-testing sessions, bringing her good cheer and years of vegan cooking experience to the task. Elizabeth Schneider, produce specialist and dear friend, generously shared her vast understanding of vegetables and how they best like to be selected, stored, and cooked. Splendid vegan dessert classes taught by Fran Costigan and Myra Kornfeld at the Natural Gourmet Cooking School were inspirational. Colleague and coffee-mate Dorie Greenspan cast her keen editorial eye over the introductory section.

Consulting and recipe development for Eden Foods, Inc. have provided an ongoing opportunity to work with superb organic soymilks, canned beans, tomatoes, pasta, and other high-quality vegan products. Jean Richardson of Gold Mine Natural Food Co. kept me posted on the ingredients she's most excited about and provided a generous supply of samples.

Thanks to Bill LeBlond for inviting me to take on this challenging project and for celebrating the bounty in living color. Gracias and besos to Richard Isaacson, who understood when I postponed our trip to Spain and who continues to be my loving and devoted companion on the bigger journey.

TABLE OF CONTENTS

INTRODUCTION

Are you trying to figure out what on earth to cook for a vegan child or friend? Or perhaps you'd like to experience an occasional vegan meal yourself?

Grains, vegetables, and fruits fill the abundant vegan pantry, but you won't find any meat, fish, eggs, cheese, or milk in sight. Since plants contain no cholesterol, vegan meals are 100 percent cholesterol free.

Understandably, many people are attracted to vegan cooking for health reasons. Others have philosophical or ecological concerns. And kosher cooks find vegan recipes appealing because they can be slipped into any type of menu. Whatever the impulse, it's clear that a growing number of Americans are choosing broccoli over beef.

Impelled by the word "new" in this book's title, I've made it my goal to create innovative dishes that everyone will eat with pleasure. The source of my inspiration has been the global kitchen, but I have made no attempt at authenticity. Rather, I offer you dishes of my own invention that celebrate the fresh and flavor-packed bounty of our good earth.

I hope that a glance at the table of contents will make you hungry and eager to join me in savoring the harvest.

HAPPY COOKING!

—LORNA SASS

CHAPTER ONE

STOCKING THE **VEGAN PANTRY**

Like a painter working from a large palette of colors, a cook takes inspiration from a pantry full of high-quality ingredients. Fortunately, most of the building blocks of vegan cooking are good keepers, and it's easy to have them on hand.

In this chapter, I've organized the ingredients into major categories and presented these categories in alphabetical order, offering relevant tips on purchasing, preparation, and storage. Once you have stocked the staples, you'll be able to cook most of the recipes. Then, little by little, you can branch out and purchase specialized ingredients for a particular dish. (Items called for only once are described in recipe headnotes rather than here.)

Although you may need to visit a health-food or gourmet shop for some of the ingredients, supermarkets are continually expanding the shelf space given to natural foods, organic produce, and specialty fare. Making requests of the grocery manager is a good way to keep this trend in motion and eventually create one-stop shopping. Mail order is also a convenient way to purchase what you can't easily find locally. For a list of my favorite mail-order sources, see page 113.

BEANS

Dried beans last indefinitely but lose flavor and moisture as they age, so shop for them in stores that have a high turnover. Look for unbroken beans with intact, brightly colored skins. Store them in airtight containers in a cool, dark place, and aim to use them within six months.

It's practical to prepare beans in quantity and freeze extra for later use. See page 19 for details and to learn about an exciting way to cook beans.

Recipes that call for cooked beans use $1^3/_4$ cups,

giving you the option of using home-cooked or canned. (A 15-ounce can holds $1^1/_2$ to $1^3/_4$ cups of drained beans.) Now that canned organic beans are so readily available, they provide a convenient preservative-free (and often salt-free) alternative to standard supermarket brands. There's no need to rinse organic beans, and you can use the canning liquid in cooking.

SUGGESTED STAPLES: black turtle beans, navy beans, chickpeas, split peas.

BRANCHING OUT: red lentils, black soybeans, cannellini beans, French Le Puy green lentils, Spanish pardina lentils, black beluga lentils, "boutique" or heirloom beans such as Christmas limas, scarlet runners, and black valentines.

BROTHS

INSTANT VEGETABLE BROTH It's convenient to have a substitute when homemade broth is not available. One reasonable option is Frontier brand vegetable broth powder, sold in bulk bins at some health-food stores and also available directly from the company (www.frontiercoop.com; 800-669-3275). The company also sells a reduced-sodium version.

Using broth instead of water is a wise choice in recipes whose success depends upon depth of flavor. Homemade broth tastes better than commercial preparations, which are usually dreadfully salty and loaded with MSG. I've included two simple recipes for homemade broths on the following pages, and you'll find a third one on page 19.

In this version, I speed up preparation by beginning to brown the onions as I chop and toss in the carrots and celery. Tomato paste gives the broth an earthy color, and a bit of salt draws out the vegetables' flavors.

Tip: A wide 2-quart Pyrex measuring cup with spout comes in very handy for collecting the broth as you pass it through a large colander or strainer.

BASIC VEGETABLE BROTH

MAKES **6 TO 8** CUPS

1 1/2 TABLESPOONS OLIVE OIL

3 MEDIUM ONIONS, DICED

3 LARGE CARROTS

2 LARGE CELERY RIBS

1 TABLESPOON TOMATO PASTE

1/2 CUP DRY WHITE WINE OR VERMOUTH

10 CUPS WATER

3 LARGE CLOVES GARLIC, CRUSHED (PEELING IS NOT NECESSARY)

STEMS FROM 1 BUNCH PARSLEY, CHOPPED

1/4 OUNCE (1/4 CUP LOOSELY PACKED) DRIED MUSHROOMS (YOU CAN USE AN INEXPENSIVE SUPERMARKET BRAND)

1/4 CUP RED LENTILS

1/4 TEASPOON DRIED THYME LEAVES

1/4 TEASPOON SALT

1/4 TEASPOON WHOLE BLACK PEPPERCORNS

01 In a 6-quart (or larger) heavy-bottomed pot, heat the oil. Add the onions and begin browning them over medium-high heat as you chop and toss in the carrots and celery. Continue cooking, stirring frequently, until the onions are nicely browned, 10 to 15 minutes. Lower the heat if the vegetables begin to burn or stick.

02 Stir in the tomato paste and cook about 30 seconds. Add the wine, stir to release any browned bits sticking to the bottom of the pot, and cook over high heat until most of the wine has evaporated, a minute or two. Add the water and remaining ingredients and bring to a boil.

03 Set the lid off-center to create a 1/4-inch steam vent. Lower the heat and simmer until the broth develops a good flavor, 1 to 1 1/2 hours. Cool, then strain through a colander set over a large bowl, pressing down the vegetables to extract as much broth as possible. Refrigerate for up to 4 days, or freeze in convenient quantities for up to 3 months.

OTHER IDEAS

Include a few leek greens and scrubbed potato peels.

Use 1/4 pound chopped fresh mushrooms (or leftover portobello stems) instead of dried.

See Bonus Bean Broth, page 19.

6 CUPS WATER OR GRAIN OR BEAN COOKING LIQUID (OR A COMBINATION)

FISTFUL OF LEEK GREENS (FROM 3 MEDIUM LEEKS), TRIMMED AND COARSELY CHOPPED

STEMS FROM 1 BUNCH PARSLEY

$1/2$ OUNCE ($1/2$ CUP LOOSELY PACKED) DRIED MUSHROOMS (USE A SUPERMARKET VARIETY, NOT YOUR BEST PORCINI OR MORELS)

1 BAY LEAF

$1/4$ TEASPOON SALT (OPTIONAL)

$1/8$ TEASPOON BLACK PEPPERCORNS

Here's a quick and dandy way to make good use of leek greens, which give up their mild and pleasing flavor with great dispatch. The broth's taste is predominantly leek, with a subtle mushroom backdrop. Use it in any recipe that calls for vegetable broth.

BUSY COOK'S **LEEK** BROTH

01 Combine the ingredients in a large pot and bring to a simmer. Set the cover slightly off-center to create a $1/4$-inch steam vent, and simmer over low heat until the broth develops a good flavor and color, 20 to 30 minutes.

02 Cool, then strain through a colander set over a large bowl, pressing down the vegetables to extract all of the liquid. Refrigerate in a tightly sealed container for up to 3 days, or freeze in convenient quantities for up to 3 months.

OTHER IDEAS

Instead of dried mushrooms, substitute a cup or two of chopped fresh mushrooms or leftover portobello stems.

Toss in a few chopped celery or fennel stalks, if you have them on hand.

NUTS AND NUT BUTTERS

With their luxurious richness and intense flavor, nuts and nut butters make a valuable contribution to vegan sauces and desserts—and a superb spread for bread. Although nuts are high in fat, most of that fat is the heart-healthy kind.

To avoid rancidity, store nut butters in the refrigerator and nuts in the freezer. Try to use them within three months.

SUGGESTED STAPLES: almonds, walnuts, pecans, almond or cashew butter, peanut butter.

BRANCHING OUT: pine nuts, hazelnuts, pistachios, hazelnut butter, sesame tahini.

TOASTING NUTS AND SEEDS Toast nuts on a baking pan in a toaster oven (most convenient) or standard oven set to 375°F until fragrant and lightly browned, 2 to 5 minutes. Stir once halfway through. Seeds can also be toasted in a skillet set over medium-high heat; stir them frequently. Nuts and seeds burn easily, so watch them closely.

OILS

For the variety and elegant finish they offer, high-quality, aromatic oils can't be beat. Although expensive, a tablespoon goes a long way. Store them in the refrigerator or in a dark, cool place, and your oils will last the better part of a year.

Unfortunately, even expensive oils vary in quality and freshness, so your best bet is to purchase them from a gourmet shop that prides itself on carrying the best. Zingerman's is a good mail-order source.

SUGGESTED STAPLES: pure olive oil for cooking and a fine extra-virgin olive oil for salads; a neutral (bland-tasting) vegetable oil such as grapeseed, corn, peanut, safflower, or canola for cooking.

BRANCHING OUT: rosemary- or basil-infused olive oil (Consorzio brand is reliably good); hazelnut oil; walnut oil (French and Italian imports tend to be superior); toasted (Asian) sesame oil; roasted peanut oil (Loriva is a good brand); organic, unrefined coconut oil (available by mail from Gold Mine Natural Food Co.) for cooking and baking.

SOYFOODS

It's hard to open a newspaper nowadays without reading about the health benefits of soy. Because I focused on these "miracle" foods in *The New Soy Cookbook,* I have featured them only occasionally in this recipe collection.

TOFU is certainly the best-known soyfood. Also called bean curd, it is prepared by coagulating soymilk in a process that resembles cheese-making. Tofu is labeled firm or soft, depending upon its water content. For stir-fries and other dishes that require the tofu to hold its shape, opt for the firm or extra-firm variety.

Soft tofu is often a better choice for sauces and dressings, since it creates a smoother purée and contains sufficient liquid to result in a pourable consistency. Most soft tofu is labeled "silken," referring to a Japanese preparation technique that results in a custardlike texture. You can use either the shelf-stable, aseptic-packed silken-soft tofu or the fresh, refrigerated variety. In either case, note the expiration date marked on the package.

Once you've opened the container, cover any leftovers with water and refrigerate in a sealed container. Change the water every other day and the tofu will remain fresh for about five days.

TEMPEH is a dense soybean cake whose taste is often described as "mushroomy" or "yeasty." In recipes, it comes across as heartier than tofu. Because tempeh is a fermented product, many people who experience difficulty digesting other soyfoods have an easy time with it.

Tempeh is typically sold in 8-ounce slabs, and you'll find it in the refrigerator or frozen-food section of your market. Tempeh made entirely of soybeans has a stronger taste than tempeh made with a mixture of soybeans and grains. You can use either type in the recipes. Cook tempeh before the expiration date, or freeze it for up to three months (assuming it hasn't already been frozen).

SOYMILK is made by simmering ground soybeans in water and then pressing out the liquid. Most soymilk is sold in shelf-stable aseptic "bricks." Since manufacturers add a variety of ingredients to enhance taste, the nutrient profile varies considerably among brands. Compare labels and sample widely before settling on a favorite. I use Eden Foods soymilk, as it is made from organic soybeans (never genetically modified) and is among the highest in protein. Once you've opened a container, soymilk remains fresh under refrigeration for at least five days.

(The soyfoods miso and soy sauce are discussed later in the Other Good Things section, page 15.)

> **SUGGESTED STAPLES:** soymilk, 12-ounce aseptic-packed silken-soft tofu.

> **BRANCHING OUT:** tempeh.

VEGETABLES

There's nothing like the color and promise of fresh vegetables to infuse the kitchen with a sense of vitality and well-being. I particularly love hearty greens and members of the onion family. For details on handling these and other vegetables, check the Veggie Prep section below.

> **SUGGESTED STAPLES:** onions, scallions (green onions), garlic, ginger, carrots, celery, salad greens.

> **BRANCHING OUT:** leeks, shallots, fennel, kale, collard greens.

VEGGIE PREP

When it comes to efficiently preparing vegetables for the pot, there's no better kitchen helper than a sharp knife. I recommend a 10-inch blade, which does a lot more of the work for you than the commonly recommended 8-inch chef's knife.

My other best prep-buddy is the Sharpery, a small, inexpensive, and cleverly designed honing device that makes your knives razor sharp in ten quick swipes. You can mail order the Sharpery from Zabar's (see page 113) or call Chantry at 800-242-6879 to locate a local source.

Following is a description of techniques needed to prepare the vegetables used in the recipes, organized into alphabetical order by ingredient.

ROASTING GARLIC Remove any loose, papery skins from a whole head of garlic. Set the whole head in a shallow baking dish in a toaster oven or standard oven and roast at 375°F until soft, 20 to 30 minutes. Use immediately or refrigerate in a sealed container for up to 10 days. Squeeze the soft flesh out of each clove as needed.

GRATING GINGER To grate ginger, use a porcelain grater, available in Asian groceries, or the side of a box grater with rice-sized holes. Better yet, use the terrific rasp sold for grating cheese, available from Cooking by the Book, Inc. (212-966-9799). It's not necessary to peel ginger before grating it, but do peel before mincing.

SELECTING AND PREPARING HEARTY GREENS When purchasing kale, collards, escarole, and other leafy greens, look for bunches with sprightly greens that are neither browned nor wilted. Chop first, then rinse or dunk to remove any sand. Although many recipes advise discarding stems and thick mid-ribs, this is not necessary: when thinly sliced, they cook up just fine.

KEEPING SALAD GREENS CRISP Wash and spin-dry the greens. Place a paper towel on the bottom of a Tupperware-style plastic container large enough to hold the greens without crushing them. Cover the container and set it in the bottom third of the refrigerator. Greens will remain crisp for 5 to 7 days. (Really!)

"WHITTLING" HERBS AND WATERCRESS To quickly cut the leaves from parsley, cilantro, dill, or watercress, try this dandy technique: Hold the bunch of herbs by the stems at a slight angle so that some of the leaves are resting on a clean, flat surface. Place a very sharp chef's knife at a 45-degree angle at the point where the leaves meet the stems. Then glide the knife toward the top of the bunch with a swift stroke. When you've removed the leaves from one section, turn the bunch and continue whittling. Some leaves will inevitably still be attached to their slender stems; pinch them off one by one only if a recipe demands such perfection. This technique doesn't work with basil, mint, and other herbs that have woody stems.

SLICING AND CLEANING LEEKS Slice off the root ends, and then slice the white and light green part, removing any bruised or tough outer layers. Rinse well, separating the rings, and release all sand hidden between the layers. Drain thoroughly. Reserve dark green leaf-tops for stock.

ZESTING LEMONS OR ORANGES Use organic fruit when available. The best tool for zesting is the rasp available from Cooking by the Book, Inc. (212-966-9799). You can also use a standard zester or the finest side of a box grater.

STORING AND CLEANING FRESH MUSHROOMS Refrigerate mushrooms in an open paper bag, and use them as soon as possible. Before use, gently brush off any dirt with a damp paper towel.

ROASTING RED PEPPERS Set peppers over a high gas flame. Rotate with tongs until thoroughly charred. (If using an electric oven, cut the peppers in half, remove the seeds, and core. Press firmly to flatten. Set cut side down under the broiler, as close to the broiling element as possible.) Wrap each pepper in a wet paper towel and enclose in a plastic bag. When cool, use the paper towels to rub off the skins. (It's okay if a few charred bits remain intact.) Core and seed the peppers. If not using immediately, toss the peppers in olive oil and refrigerate them in a tightly sealed container.

WHOLE GRAINS

I enjoy the go-down-easiness of white rice, and basmati usually comes to mind when I'm serving Indian food, but for providing a sense of satiety, there is nothing quite like chewy whole grains. I encourage you to try the easy, foolproof technique for cooking and storing them described on pages 20–22.

To avoid rancidity, freeze raw whole grains in well-sealed containers. (I use zipper-topped plastic freezer bags, which can easily be tucked into nooks and crannies.) Although frozen grains will last a year or more, I try to use them within six months.

SUGGESTED STAPLES: short-grain brown rice, basmati rice, pearl barley, wheat berries.

BRANCHING OUT: wild rice, Colusari red rice, kamut, hulled barley, black buffalo barley, quinoa.

OTHER GOOD THINGS

BREWER'S YEAST Don't let its unappealing name get in your way; this fine-tasting, nutritious powder adds savory depth and a hint of Parmesan cheese flavor to vegan dishes. The best-tasting brewer's yeast I've found is made by Lewis Laboratories. Look for it in the supplements section of health-food stores, or call 800-243-6020. Opt for the powder rather than buds or flakes, and don't substitute another brand unless you like the way it tastes.

CHOCOLATE AND COCOA POWDER Many brands of unsweetened cocoa powder and dark chocolate are vegan (check the labels), and numerous organic brands are available in health-food stores. Tropical Source produces tasty espresso and chocolate chips. Scharffen Berger makes particularly fine cocoa powder and baking chocolate (www.scharffen-berger.com).

HERBS AND SPICES Some lucky folks live near health-food stores that sell dried herbs and spices in bulk bins, making it possible to purchase small quantities. This is ideal, since dried herbs in particular lose their vitality after about six months. (You can mail order small quantities from Penzeys, page 113.)

You can purchase mixtures of Italian or Provençal herbs in bottles, but it's fun and more economical to make your own. Be sure to use dried herb leaves, not ground.

TWO **HERB** BLENDS

MAKES ABOUT 1/4 CUP EACH

ITALIAN HERB BLEND

1 TABLESPOON DRIED OREGANO

1 TABLESPOON DRIED BASIL

2 TEASPOONS DRIED THYME

2 TEASPOONS DRIED ROSEMARY

1 1/2 TEASPOONS FENNEL SEEDS

1 TEASPOON CRUSHED RED PEPPER FLAKES (OPTIONAL)

HERBES DE PROVENCE

1 TABLESPOON DRIED BASIL

2 TEASPOONS DRIED TARRAGON

2 TEASPOONS DRIED SAVORY

2 TEASPOONS DRIED ROSEMARY

2 TEASPOONS DRIED MARJORAM

2 TEASPOONS DRIED CHERVIL (OPTIONAL)

Combine the herbs for either blend in a small, wide-mouthed jar. Shake well. Store in a dark, cool place for up to 6 months.

Store dried herbs and spices away from heat and light. For optimum flavor, buy whole spices and grind them just before use in a coffee grinder set aside for this purpose or with a mortar and pestle.

My favorite store-bought curry blend is Merwanjee Poonjiajee & Sons Madras Curry Powder, sold in small tins in many gourmet shops and Indian groceries (and available by mail from Zabar's). It is a mild blend that you can punch up, if you wish, by adding cayenne. I used this brand in all recipe testing and, since it contains salt, you may need to make adjustments if using another curry blend.

MAPLE SYRUP Opt for pure maple syrup, and avoid any products that contain corn syrup and artificial coloring. Grade A Dark Amber has the most flavor.

MISO Miso is a thick paste made by fermenting soybeans or a combination of soybeans and grains. In general, dark misos are saltier and have a more intense, "beefy" flavor than light misos. Dissolve miso in liquid before adding it to your dish. Look for miso in the refrigerated section of health-food stores and Asian markets (or order by mail from Gold Mine Natural Food Co., page 113). Miso Master is a good brand. Refrigerate miso in a tightly sealed container, and it will last for years.

SALT I favor sea salt because I like its taste and the fact that it has trace minerals. Sea salt from the Atlantic coast of Brittany is excellent. (Supermarket salt contains additives that are not health-promoting, so I avoid it.) Measurements assume that you are using finely ground salt.

SOY SAUCE Much of the soy sauce sold in this country is made with artificial ingredients and is of very poor quality. I recommend traditionally brewed, imported Japanese soy sauces—either tamari or shoyu—which have more complex flavor and are less assertively salty than Chinese soy sauces. Eden Foods and Ohsawa, both sold in health-food stores, are good brands. Eden has a reduced-sodium version. Refrigerate opened bottles or store them in a cool place, and they will last for at least a year.

SUGAR Those who prefer organic and strictly vegan products (charcoal made from animal bone is used in some sugar refinement processes) can now find various brands of dehydrated cane juice in health-food stores. Any of these products can be used instead of standard sugar.

VINEGARS AND CITRUS JUICES When I need an acid to sharpen the flavor of a dish or to prepare a salad dressing, I usually opt for the vibrant freshness of lemon or lime juice. There are times, however, when a good vinegar is the better choice.

A touch of aged, mellow balsamic vinegar added after cooking melds the tastes of individual ingredients and adds a subtle layer of sweetness, resulting in a dish that is more satisfying. My favorite balsamic is Cavalli, available in gourmet shops and by mail order from Zabar's and Zingerman's (see page 113). An excellent substitute is balsamic syrup, which you can easily make at home from an inexpensive brand. (See Balsamic Syrup recipe on page 16.)

> **SUGGESTED STAPLES:** lemons, limes, good-quality balsamic vinegar.

> **BRANCHING OUT:** raspberry vinegar, sherry vinegar, Balsamic Syrup.

A teaspoon or two of balsamic syrup can magically transform a ho-hum dish into something that you want to savor slowly. Fortunately, it is easy to make. However, be sure to open all of the kitchen windows and turn on the exhaust before you begin: the process creates potent fumes.

BALSAMIC SYRUP

MAKES ⅓ CUP

1 CUP BALSAMIC VINEGAR (SUPERMARKET QUALITY IS FINE)

Pour the vinegar into a small, heavy, nonreactive saucepan, preferably one with a pouring spout. Bring to a boil over high heat. Reduce the heat and cook at a moderate boil until thickened and reduced to about ⅓ cup, about 12 minutes. Cool in the pot, and then pour into a small glass jar and store at room temperature. Lasts indefinitely.

2

CHAPTER TWO

NEW WAYS WITH **BEANS** AND **GRAINS**

1 POUND (ABOUT 2 ½ CUPS) DRIED BEANS, PICKED OVER AND RINSED

1 TEASPOON SALT, PREFERABLY SEA SALT

BOILING WATER TO COVER BEANS BY 2 INCHES

Over the past decade, I've experimented with various ways to cook beans and grains. Assuming that you can find standard approaches in any basic cookbook, I'm using this space to describe two less common techniques that I'm excited about.

For beans that hold their shape perfectly and have an intensely creamy texture, try slow-baking them in the oven, and you will be amazed. Although the process may take as long as three hours, almost no work is involved. Since slow-baked beans hold their flavor and shape very nicely when frozen, it's practical to make a large quantity for later use.

I was convinced to try slow-baking beans while reading and cooking from Sylvia Thompson's The Kitchen Garden Cookbook, a fresh and fetching collection of recipes I heartily recommend. Thompson credits Russ Parsons of the Los Angeles Times for introducing her to this fine technique. I thank them both, and you will too.

By eliminating presoaking and adding salt right from the start, the cooked beans develop maximum flavor, maintain good color, and end up with their glossy skins intact. Especially when seasoned with the ingredients for a Bonus Bean Broth (see opposite), they are tasty enough to serve as a simple side dish, tossed lightly with olive oil or garnished with fresh herbs.

For a special treat, try this technique with some of the unusual boutique beans now on the market—or slow-bake large limas, which end up looking like suitable fare for Gargantua. For advice on purchasing and storing dried beans, see page 8.

SLOW-BAKED BEANS

01 Place a rack in the center of the oven and preheat to 250°F.

02 Set the beans in a large Dutch oven or lidded casserole. Sprinkle with salt. Pour enough boiling water over them to cover by 2 inches. Cover and bake until the beans are tender, 1 to 4 hours, depending on size and condition. (Most beans take 2 to 3 hours, but an occasional batch can surprise you.) Add boiling water, if needed, to keep the beans covered.

03 If you like the way the cooking liquid tastes, reserve it when you drain the beans. Refrigerate the beans for up to 3 days, or freeze until needed (see Freezing Cooked Beans opposite).

FREEZING COOKED BEANS

After the beans have cooled, freeze them in heavy, zipper-topped plastic bags. It's convenient to store them in $1^3/_4$-cup quantities, the approximate amount contained in a 15-ounce can, and the amount I call for in recipes. Defrost frozen beans either at room temperature or in a microwave.

BONUS BEAN BROTH

Cook the beans with 1 chunked carrot, 2 sliced celery ribs, 1 large bay leaf, 1 halved shallot or small onion, 1 or 2 crushed cloves of garlic (optional), and $1/_8$ teaspoon peppercorns. Remove and discard the vegetables after draining the beans. Use the broth for soups and stews.

Make a tasty side dish or a spread for baguette by mashing the cooked beans coarsely with roasted garlic and olive oil. Season well with salt and pepper.

Garnish the beans with Gremolata (page 63).

See the recipe for Slow-Baked Cannellini with Olives, Escarole, and Gremolata (page 63) for another approach to this technique.

3 QUARTS WATER

1 TEASPOON SALT (OPTIONAL)

**1 POUND (ABOUT 2 ½ CUPS) WHOLE
GRAINS**

FEARLESS WHOLE-GRAIN COOKERY

Cook whole grains like pasta in an abundance of boiling water. When they are tender, drain the grains and steam them in the hot, covered pot for a few minutes. You'll end up with perfectly cooked morsels every time.

I first read about this method in The Cook's Bible *by Christopher Kimball and have been happily experimenting with it ever since. The approach successfully deals with the reality that no two batches of grains absorb exactly the same amount of liquid. Because the pot is open during cooking, you can easily taste for doneness along the way—a great boon since timing can vary widely depending upon harvesting conditions and freshness.*

No more scorched pots! As if that weren't enough, this technique often cuts down cooking time by 5 or 10 minutes. Are you sold?

Use this recipe for pearl, hulled, and black buffalo barley; wheat or rye berries; wild rice; kamut; quinoa; millet; Colusari red rice; and short-grain brown rice. It's not necessary to rinse grains before cooking except in the case of quinoa. See Grain Cooking Times (opposite) for timing and comments specific to individual grains.

Since cooked grains freeze so well, this recipe calls for preparing 1 pound of dried grains at a time, with the idea of storing leftovers for later use (see Freezing Cooked Grain, page 22).

BASIC GRAINS

01 In a 6-quart (or larger) pot, bring the water, salt (if using), and grains to a boil. Cook uncovered at a moderate boil, stirring occasionally to prevent any grains from sticking to the bottom of the pot. Add more boiling water, if necessary, to keep the grains covered.

02 When the grains are tender (see Grain Cooking Times for approximate cooking times), drain thoroughly. (Taste the cooking liquid before draining and, if you like it, set the strainer over a bowl to reserve the liquid for future use.) Bounce the strainer up and down to shake as much water off the grains as you can. Immediately transfer the grains back to the hot pot. Cover the pot and set aside off heat to steam and dry out the grains, 8 to 10 minutes. (If the grains are quite tender and you are fearful of overcooking them, skip this step.)

03 Fluff up the grains before serving. Refrigerate any reserved cooking liquid and use within 24 hours, or freeze for up to 3 months.

GRAIN COOKING TIMES

Cook grains just a tad short of tender, since they will steam for a few more minutes after you drain them. Keep in mind that some whole grains, such as short-grain brown rice, kamut, and wheat berries, remain chewy even when thoroughly cooked.

BARLEY (BLACK BUFFALO OR HULLED)	35 to 45 minutes	Black buffalo is a large, dark grain; striking in a medley
BARLEY (PEARL)	25 to 35 minutes	Accommodates well to cooking with other grains
BROWN RICE (SHORT-GRAIN)	35 to 40 minutes	Texture and taste far superior to long-grain varieties
COLUSARI RED RICE	20 to 25 minutes	Holds color nicely; a good alternative to wild rice
KAMUT	45 minutes	A large, buttery grain; highly recommended
MILLET	12 to 15 minutes	Dry-toast (see Other Ideas, page 22) before boiling; turns to mush if over-cooked
QUINOA	12 to 14 minutes	Before cooking, swish in several changes of water to remove natural bitter coating
WHEAT BERRIES (HARD WHEAT)	50 to 60 minutes	A small, dense, and chewy grain best used in medleys
WILD RICE (PRESOAKED)	35 to 45 minutes	Presoaking for a few hours or overnight results in more even cooking but is not essential when cooking in a medley

OTHER IDEAS

DRY-TOASTING GRAINS Dry-toasting gives grains a hint of nuttiness and usually shaves a few minutes off the boiling time. I consider dry-toasting optional except in the case of millet, whose taste and texture are considerably improved by taking this extra step.

To dry-toast grains, place the uncooked grains in a large, nonstick skillet set over medium heat. Once the skillet is hot, stir or shake the grains almost constantly until they emit a strong, toasted fragrance, turn a shade darker, or begin to pop (whichever happens first), 2 to 5 minutes. If the grains begin to scorch, immediately transfer them out of the skillet. Allow the toasted grains to cool before further cooking.

FREEZING COOKED GRAINS When the grains are cool, transfer them to storage containers or freezer-weight reclosable bags in convenient quantities, such as 1- or 2-cup portions. If you need less than the amount of frozen grains in any bag, simply bang the bag gently against the kitchen counter to release the amount you need.

REHYDRATING AND REHEATING REFRIGERATED OR FROZEN GRAINS
Leftover grains become dry and brittle after an overnight sojourn in the refrigerator. The microwave does an impressive job of revitalizing them. Simply place the refrigerated or frozen cooked grains in a strainer and rinse under hot water. Transfer to a bowl, cover lightly with a paper towel or waxed paper, and microwave until piping hot. (You'll probably have to stir once or twice to reheat the grains evenly.)

If you don't own a microwave, steam the grains over hot water.

GRAIN MEDLEYS For textural and visual variety, try boiling a few different grains together. Start by selecting grains that have approximately the same cooking times. Short-grain brown rice and barley are excellent together in a ratio of 3 to 1. A small handful of wild rice, Colusari red rice, or black barley adds nice color to the mix.

If you are a risk-taker, you can give longer-cooking grains a head start in the pot and then add shorter-cooking grains at appropriate intervals. For example, start with wheat berries and then add short-grain brown rice 15 minutes later. Alternatively, if you soak the wheat berries overnight, you can cook them with the brown rice right from the start.

Whole grains are more forgiving than white rice or pasta, and most offer a 10-minute window of chewiness before tasting waterlogged and overcooked. But use this approach only if you have tolerance for occasional imperfection. (Avoid combos with quinoa and millet, as these grains quickly turn to mush if overcooked.) A safer way to create grain medleys is to cook and freeze each type of grain separately. Combine and heat them as the spirit moves you.

SEASONING GRAINS Coat grains very lightly with your finest olive, nut, or herb-infused oil (or a combination).

Toss grains with finely chopped fresh herbs and/or toasted seeds or chopped nuts.

See the recipe for Savory Grains on page 84.

3

DESIGNING **VEGAN MENUS**

With this book in hand, planning dinner couldn't be easier: most of the recipes in the Main Course chapter can be served on their own, and everyone will walk away from the table feeling satisfied. To design a more complex meal, first select the main course. Then follow the suggestions for accompaniments offered in the recipe's introduction. Alternatively, skim through the book and select a companion dish that suits your mood.

Two good ways to expand a meal are to serve grains with a vegetable entrée or beans with a grain-based main dish. See pages 18 to 22 for ways to keep cooked grains and beans on hand and ideas for dressing them up at the last minute.

Keep in mind that when dishes contain no animal protein, portions tend to be about 20 percent larger. I've taken this into account when estimating servings and have erred on the side of providing too much rather than too little.

Here are some themed menu possibilities and a few quick-reference lists. An item in parentheses indicates that I've provided no specific recipe and am leaving the creative details to you.

MEDITERRANEAN FEAST

Hiziki Tapenade

Slow-Baked Cannellini with Olives, Escarole, and Gremolata

Slow-Roasted Tomatoes and Fennel

Pine Nut–Anise Crescents

PASSAGE TO INDIA

Skillet Grain Medley with Curried Tempeh or Tomato-Chickpea Curry in Eggplant Shells

Cucumber-Mint "Raita"

Carrot Slaw with Mango Chutney Dressing

Mango-Coconut Tapioca

COMPANY IS COMING

Mediterranean Red Lentil Pâté

Stuffed Collard Rolls with Roasted Red Pepper Sauce

(Radicchio and Endive Salad) with Creamy Herb Dressing

Rustic Apple Tart

ASIAN MEDLEY

Split-Pea Soup with Shiitake and Star Anise

Brussels Sprouts and Udon Noodles in Miso Sauce

(Napa Cabbage Slaw) with Sesame-Watercress Dressing

(Pineapple Chunks Tossed with Canned Lichees)

SIMPLE SOUP MEAL

Roasted Sweet Potato and Corn Chowder

(Wholegrain Bread or Crackers with Almond, Cashew, or Hazelnut Butter)

(Tossed Green Salad) with Creamy Herb Dressing

FAST LUNCH OR SUPPER IDEAS

As-You-Please Grain and Bean Salad

Portobello "Steaks" with (Baked Potatoes) or (Tossed Green Salad) with Creamy Herb Dressing

Thai-Inspired Broccoli in Coconut-Cilantro Sauce

Crisp Tortilla Stacks with Roasted Corn and Black Beans

Black Soybean and Vegetable "Sushi"

LUNCHBOX FARE

Black Soybean and Vegetable "Sushi"

Mediterranean Red Lentil Pâté in Pita

Portobello "Steak" Sandwich

As-You-Please Grain and Bean Salad

Baked Beet and Brown Rice Salad

BREAKFAST AND BRUNCH IDEAS

Wholegrain Waffles

Sweet Polenta with Maple-Glazed Walnuts

Phyllo Triangles filled with Kale, Pine Nuts, and Currants

Rustic Apple Tart

QUICK DESSERT OPTIONS

Chocolate Rice Pudding

Sweet Polenta with Maple-Glazed Walnuts

(Dairy-free Ice Cream or Sorbet)

CHAPTER FOUR

STARTERS, SOUPS, AND LITTLE MEALS

1 OUNCE HIZIKI (ALSO SPELLED HIJIKI)

1 SMALL CLOVE GARLIC, PEELED

1/2 CUP PITTED, OIL-CURED BLACK OLIVES (SAVE TIME BY BUYING THEM ALREADY PITTED)

3 TABLESPOONS DRAINED CAPERS (PACKED IN BRINE)

2 TABLESPOONS OLIVE OIL, PLUS MORE IF NEEDED

1 TO 2 TABLESPOONS FRESHLY SQUEEZED LEMON JUICE

SALT (OPTIONAL)

FRESH THYME LEAVES, FOR GARNISH

Tapenade is a heady Provençal blend of olives, capers, and anchovies. In this version, I've used the mildly briny, jet-black sea vegetable called hiziki instead of anchovies. The result is a bold and rustic dip for raw vegetables or chips and a memorable spread for bread or wafer-thin rice crackers.

It's wise to purchase the hiziki in a health-food store, where the quality is likely to be better than you'll find in an Asian market. During processing, hiziki's large leaves are shredded and dried in such a tangle that it's impossible to give you a dry-cup measurement. If you don't have a kitchen scale, just "guesstimate" for now. Then please go out and buy one.

HIZIKI TAPENADE

01 Place the hiziki in a large bowl and pour enough boiling water on top to cover it by 2 inches. Let sit until tender and pliable, 10 to 20 minutes, stirring once or twice. Drain thoroughly.

02 With the motor of the food processor running, pop the garlic into the feed tube and chop. Add the hiziki, olives, capers, and oil. Process to create a coarse paste, scraping down the sides of the bowl as needed.

03 Add enough lemon juice and salt, if needed, to give the tapenade an assertive flavor. (The amount you'll need will depend upon the saltiness and flavor of the olives and capers; I've added as much as 1 teaspoon of salt and 2 tablespoons of lemon juice.)

04 If serving as a dip, thin the mixture slightly with olive oil, if necessary. Transfer to a bowl and garnish with thyme.

OTHER IDEAS

For a pleasing appetizer, set small mounds of tapenade in the center of plates and surround them with Slow-Roasted Tomatoes and Fennel (page 80). Serve with sliced, toasted baguette.

Use a tablespoon or two of tapenade as a flavor booster in soups and stews.

Thin the tapenade with olive oil and/or a tablespoon or two of pasta cooking-water, and toss with hot pasta. Add chopped fresh thyme, parsley, or basil, if you wish.

2 TABLESPOONS OLIVE OIL, PLUS MORE FOR OILING RAMEKINS OR LOAF PANS

3 TABLESPOONS TOASTED SUN-FLOWER SEEDS OR CHOPPED PISTACHIOS

1 ½ CUPS FINELY DICED ONIONS

1 CUP FINELY DICED SHALLOTS

1 TEASPOON FENNEL SEEDS, GENTLY CRUSHED IN A MORTAR OR UNDER A CHEF'S KNIFE

½ TEASPOON DRIED THYME LEAVES

1 LARGE CLOVE GARLIC, MINCED

1 TABLESPOON TOMATO PASTE

¼ CUP DRY WHITE WINE OR VERMOUTH

3 CUPS WATER

1 ½ CUPS RED LENTILS, PICKED OVER AND RINSED

1 BAY LEAF

1 TEASPOON SALT

FRESHLY GROUND BLACK PEPPER

ACCOMPANIMENTS: OLIVES, SLOW-ROASTED TOMATOES AND FENNEL (PAGE 80), CORNICHONS, PICKLED ONIONS, MARINATED ARTICHOKE HEARTS, OR MUSHROOMS

A FEW PARSLEY LEAVES, FOR GARNISH

Red lentils seasoned with Mediterranean herbs quickly melt down into a savory purée. (Some people have been observed spreading a hot spoonful of it onto bread.) When chilled, the mixture firms up into an elegant pâté. Like most pâtés, this one ages and keeps well, so you can count on enjoying it for a week or more.

Use either two 2-cup mini-loaf pans or 8 individual ½-cup ramekins for chilling the pâté. If using loaf pans, unmold the pâté and serve it whole on a buffet platter, or set slices on individual plates. Either unmold the ramekins or serve individual portions right in them.

For an appetizer or light lunch, serve the pâté with a small salad of mixed greens and a variety of the intensely flavored accompaniments suggested below. And, of course, a sliced baguette.

You'll find red lentils in health-food stores, most supermarkets, and in Indian groceries, where they are called masoor dal. Be forewarned that heat turns these lovely red lentils yellowish tan, a reminder that cooking is chemistry—or should I say alchemy?

MEDITERRANEAN **RED LENTIL** PÂTÉ

01 Brush oil on the bottom and sides of the loaf pans or ramekins. Sprinkle sunflower seeds on the bottom. Set aside.

02 In a large, heavy, nonreactive pot, heat the oil. Cook the onions and shallots over medium-high heat, stirring frequently, until golden brown, 6 to 8 minutes. Stir in the fennel, thyme, garlic, and tomato paste and cook, stirring constantly, for about 30 seconds. Add the wine and scrape up any browned bits sticking to the bottom of the pot. Cook until most of the wine evaporates, about 30 seconds.

03 Add the water, lentils, and bay leaf and bring to a boil. Cover and simmer, stirring occasionally, for 20 minutes. Add the salt and pepper and continue cooking until the lentils have melted into a coarse purée, 10 to 20 minutes longer. Remove the bay leaf and adjust the seasonings. (Be sure there's enough salt.)

04 Stir well, smashing any whole lentils onto the sides of the pot to create a fairly smooth, thick mixture, with a texture similar to oatmeal. If the purée is loose and soupy, boil it uncovered, stirring frequently, until it thickens.

05 Ladle the purée immediately into the oiled loaf pans or ramekins. Smooth the top with a spatula. Cool to room temperature. Cover and chill for at least 2 hours.

06 If you want to unmold the pâté, first run a knife along the edges. Then set a plate on top, turn both loaf pan and plate over, and pray. (Actually I've never had a problem.) Bring the pâté to room temperature. Arrange on a platter or individual plates with accompaniments. Press a few parsley leaves into the seed-strewn top.

OTHER IDEAS

Stuff pâté into a pita or use it to make a focaccia sandwich. Add some shredded radicchio or arugula leaves.

Thin leftovers into a soup by stirring in tomato juice. Adjust seasonings and garnish with parsley.

Serve the pâté freshly cooked and still warm and runny, in small bowls as a starchy vegetable side dish akin to a dal.

Make these unconventional sushi by spreading a flavor-packed black soybean paste on tortillas. Top with a sheet of nori, the sea vegetable commonly used to wrap traditional sushi. Then pile on strips of carrot, cucumber, and red bell pepper, and roll the tortillas up. Slice them on an angle to expose pretty pinwheels with bright splashes of color. They make good finger food or a pleasing appetizer or light lunch. (See Other Ideas.)

Organic black soybeans have much better flavor and texture than the beige variety and are available in cans. Look for Eden brand in health-food stores, where you'll also find the other ingredients. (Or try an Asian market for the nori and condiments.) The soybean spread can be prepared a few days in advance, but the "sushi" taste best when freshly assembled.

BLACK SOYBEAN AND VEGETABLE "SUSHI"

MAKES **20 TO 24** PIECES OF "SUSHI"

BLACK SOYBEAN SPREAD

ONE 15-OUNCE CAN ORGANIC BLACK SOYBEANS, DRAINED (RESERVE LIQUID)

1 TABLESPOON TOASTED (ASIAN) SESAME OIL

1 TABLESPOON JAPANESE SOY SAUCE (SHOYU OR TAMARI), PLUS MORE IF NEEDED

2 TABLESPOONS PICKLED GINGER, PLUS MORE IF NEEDED

CHILI OIL TO TASTE (OPTIONAL)

"SUSHI"

4 SHEETS NORI (SOMETIMES LABELED SUSHI NORI)

4 TORTILLAS, 8 TO 9 INCHES IN DIAMETER (WHOLE WHEAT ARE NICE)

1 CUP FINELY SHREDDED RED CABBAGE

8 STRIPS RED BELL PEPPER, ABOUT 1/4 INCH WIDE

8 CARROT STICKS, ABOUT 1/8 INCH IN DIAMETER AND 5 INCHES LONG

1 KIRBY (PICKLING) CUCUMBER, HALVED LENGTHWISE, SEEDED, AND CUT INTO 8 STICKS ABOUT 1/4 INCH IN DIAMETER

SPRIGS OF WATERCRESS, FOR GARNISH

01 To make the Black Soybean Spread: In a food processor, combine the ingredients for the spread. Blend in enough of the reserved bean liquid (usually 1 to 2 tablespoons) to create a thick but spreadable paste. Add more soy sauce and/or pickled ginger, if needed, to give the spread an assertive taste. Season with chili oil, if you wish.

02 To assemble the "Sushi": Stack the nori and use kitchen scissors to trim the sheets into circles about 1/2 inch smaller than the tortillas.

03 Spread 2 tablespoons of the soybean mixture onto one of the tortillas, leaving a 1-inch border all around. Distribute 1/4 cup of the shredded cabbage over the bean spread. Gently press a piece of nori on top. Spread another 2 tablespoons of the soybean mixture on the nori. Set 2 red pepper strips horizontally about 1 inch from the bottom of the tortilla. Arrange 2 carrot and 2 cucumber sticks in a cluster on top.

04 Wrap the bottom edge of the tortilla over the vegetables and roll up tightly. If necessary, moisten the top edge of the tortilla lightly with soybean paste or water to seal. Gently press the roll to shape it into an even log. Proceed to fill and roll the remaining tortillas.

05 To slice the "Sushi": Set each roll on a cutting board seam side down, and use a very sharp knife to trim off the edges. Holding the

CONTINUED

roll firmly with one hand, use a gentle sawing motion of the knife to cut the roll into 5 or 6 pieces, making every other cut on the diagonal. Arrange the pieces flat side down on a platter. Garnish with watercress sprigs.

OTHER IDEAS

Instead of tortillas, use a rectangular flatbread, such as Garden of Eatin's Thin Thin Wraps, available in natural-food stores.

For a light luncheon entrée, cut each roll in half on the diagonal and lean one piece against the other in a criss-cross on a plate. Accompany with a green salad tossed with Sesame-Watercress Dressing (page 94).

Don't cut the roll, and serve it as a wrap.

Thin the spread with a few more tablespoons of bean liquid and use it as a dip for raw vegetables.

Use a pickle instead of the cucumber.

Serve the spread on wafer-thin rice crackers.

Tear the trimmed-off nori into tiny bits and use as a garnish for grains, soups, or salads.

This recipe is simplicity itself. When you have homemade vegetable broth on hand, use it to prepare this simple and restorative soup, made by infusing the broth with the earthy scent of porcini.

In The Italian Country Table, Lynne Rossetto Kasper reports that a simple broth like this is known in that country of knowledgeable eaters as an aristomaco, or tummy opener. I can also attest that the bouillon will warm you up quickly on a bone-chilling day.

The bouillon looks especially pretty when served in shallow, white soup bowls, garnished with a few snippets of chive.

PORCINI BOUILLON

SERVES 2

1 1/2 CUPS BOILING WATER

1/2 OUNCE (GENEROUS 1/2 CUP, LOOSELY PACKED) DRIED PORCINI

1/4 TEASPOON SALT, PLUS MORE IF NEEDED

2 CUPS HOMEMADE VEGETABLE OR LEEK BROTH (PAGES 9 TO 10)

SNIPPED CHIVES, FOR GARNISH (OPTIONAL)

01 Pour the boiling water into a glass liquid measuring cup and press the dried porcini into the water. Cover and let steep until the porcini are soft enough to chop, usually about 10 minutes.

02 Lift the porcini out of the water with a slotted spoon, and coarsely chop any large pieces. (Set the soaking liquid aside.) Heat a large nonstick skillet. Add the porcini and immediately sprinkle them with salt. Cook over medium-high heat, stirring constantly, until the porcini turn a shade darker and develop more intense flavor, 30 to 60 seconds. Pour in the soaking liquid, taking care to leave behind any grit that has settled on the bottom of the cup. Boil vigorously over high heat until the liquid is reduced by about half, 2 to 3 minutes.

03 Pour the vegetable broth into a saucepan and heat. Add the porcini mixture and heat thoroughly. Add salt to taste. Simmer until the broth is infused with porcini flavor, about 3 minutes. Ladle the broth through a fine sieve into bowls or cups, pressing the porcini to release all liquid. Garnish with chives, if you wish.

OTHER IDEAS

Toss the leftover soaked porcini into your next batch of rice or Savory Grains. They have little or no flavor, but their texture is pleasant, so why throw them away?

Cook grains in the bouillon. Use it as a base for soup or stew.

$3/4$ OUNCE DRIED SHIITAKE (ABOUT
10 SMALL)

2 WHOLE STAR ANISE "FLOWERS"

2 CUPS BOILING WATER, PLUS
4 CUPS ADDITIONAL WATER

1 TABLESPOON PEANUT OIL (LORIVA
BRAND ROASTED IS ESPECIALLY
GOOD)

5 SCALLIONS, THINLY SLICED (KEEP
WHITE AND GREEN PARTS
SEPARATE)

1 CUP FINELY DICED ONION

2 TEASPOONS MINCED GARLIC

$1/4$ CUP DRY SHERRY

$1 1/2$ CUPS SPLIT PEAS, PICKED OVER
AND RINSED

$1/2$ TEASPOON SALT

5-INCH CHUNK FRESH GINGER
(ABOUT 4 OUNCES)

2 TO *3* CUPS LOOSELY PACKED
WATERCRESS LEAVES (FROM
1 AVERAGE BUNCH)

1 TO *3* TABLESPOONS JAPANESE SOY
SAUCE (SHOYU OR TAMARI)

$1 1/2$ TO *3* TEASPOONS ASIAN
(TOASTED) SESAME OIL (OPTIONAL)

1 TABLESPOON TOASTED BLACK
SESAME SEEDS, FOR GARNISH
(OPTIONAL)

Dried shiitake mushrooms provide depth of flavor and star anise lends its unique tangle of licorice, resin, and smokiness to this Asian-inspired split-pea soup. Ginger juice and watercress leaves offer bright finishes of taste and color to the soothing, familiar backdrop of split peas.

The generous supply of meaty shiitake makes this soup substantial enough to serve as the main course. Opt for small shiitake—with dried caps no more than 1 inch across—if you can find them, as they rehydrate quickly. (About 10 of this size weigh $3/4$ ounce). If using larger ones, you may need to soak them longer; chop them into bite-sized morsels. You'll find dried shiitake and star anise in Asian groceries and in some health-food stores.

If you own a pressure cooker, by all means use it to make this soup. Twelve minutes under pressure melts the split peas down into a purée.

SPLIT-PEA SOUP WITH SHIITAKE AND STAR ANISE

01 Place the shiitake and star anise in a large glass measuring cup and pour the 2 cups boiling water over them. Cover and set aside until the mushrooms are tender enough to cut, usually about 10 minutes. Lift out mushrooms and star anise with a slotted spoon. Slice the caps thinly, discarding any stems (they are too woody to eat) as you go. Set the shiitake, star anise, and soaking liquid aside.

02 Heat the oil in a large soup pot. Add the white part of the sliced scallions, the onion, and the garlic, and cook over medium-high heat, stirring frequently, until they soften slightly, about 2 minutes. Add the sherry and cook over high heat, stirring constantly, until the sherry evaporates, about 30 seconds. Add the 4 cups of water, split peas, sliced shiitake, star anise (discard any broken pieces), and salt. Pour in the shiitake soaking liquid, taking care to leave behind any grit on the bottom of the cup.

03 Cover and bring to a boil. Cook at a gentle boil, stirring from time to time, until most of the peas have lost their shape, 50 to 60 minutes (or longer if the split peas are old and dried out). Taste the soup from time to time and remove the star anise if you feel it has given off sufficient flavor.

04 While the soup is cooking, prepare the ginger juice: Trim and grate the ginger (see page 13). Once you have about a tablespoon, press

the wad firmly between your fingertips and thumbs and collect the juice in a small bowl. Discard the ginger pulp. Continue grating ginger and expressing juice until you have 1 tablespoon of ginger juice. (The juice will look cloudy; some chunks of ginger are juicier than others, so you may have some ginger left over.) Set aside.

05 When the soup is done, remove the star anise "flowers." Stir well to dissolve the peas in the liquid and thicken the soup. For a creamier texture, purée part of the soup with a standard or immersion blender.

06 Just before serving, stir in the watercress and scallion greens. Add ginger juice, soy sauce, and toasted sesame oil (if using) to taste. Cook just until the watercress is wilted and tender, usually a matter of seconds. To serve, divide among 3 or 4 bowls and sprinkle with sesame seeds, if you wish.

OTHER IDEAS

Consider making the Sesame-Watercress Dressing (page 94) with the watercress stems. Toss the dressing with a slaw of shredded Chinese cabbage, carrots, and scallions for a side salad.

Replace the watercress with mesclun or chopped spinach leaves.

Instead of stirring the ginger juice into the soup, serve it in a small bowl and invite each person to add it according to personal taste.

2 MEDIUM SWEET POTATOES (ABOUT 1 POUND), PEELED AND CUT INTO 1/2-INCH DICE

2 TABLESPOONS CORN OIL (SPECTRUM NATURAL HAS A GOOD CORN TASTE)

SALT AND FRESHLY GROUND PEPPER

1 POUND FROZEN (RINSED AND DEFROSTED) OR FRESH CORN KERNELS (ABOUT 4 CUPS)

1 CUP WATER

1 1/2 CUPS FINELY DICED CELERY

1 CUP DICED RED ONION

1/4 CUP DICED SHALLOTS

1 TABLESPOON TOMATO PASTE

1/2 TEASPOON DRIED THYME LEAVES

3 CUPS VEGETABLE BROTH

1 BAY LEAF

1 RUSSET (BAKING) POTATO (ABOUT 8 OUNCES)

2 TABLESPOONS MINCED PARSLEY

1/2 TO 1 CUP UNFLAVORED SOYMILK (OPTIONAL)

This cheery chowder has a satisfying, long-cooked taste. Roasting the sweet potatoes intensifies their flavor, and puréeing most of the corn kernels instantly creates a creamy broth. I've had excellent results using frozen organic corn. Cascadian Farms and Tree of Life are two good brands.

To streamline cooking, begin preparing the soup while the sweet potatoes are roasting. If the chowder becomes too thick, stir in soymilk to thin it while adding richness and flavor.

ROASTED **SWEET POTATO** AND **CORN** CHOWDER

01 Set the oven rack in the center and preheat the oven to 425°F. Oil a large roasting pan.

02 Scatter the sweet potatoes in one layer in the roasting pan and drizzle with 1 tablespoon of the oil. Season well with salt and pepper. Roast until tender, tossing once or twice, 15 to 20 minutes. If you'd like to brown the sweet potatoes more deeply, set them about 5 inches below the broiling element for a minute or two. Set aside.

03 Reserve 1 cup of corn kernels. In a blender, purée the remaining corn with the water until very smooth, about 2 minutes. (If the corn kernel skins refuse to break down, and they look unsightly to you, pass the mixture through a sieve.) Set aside.

04 In a heavy soup pot, heat the remaining tablespoon of oil. Cook the celery, onion, and shallots over medium-high heat, stirring frequently, until the onions are slightly softened, about 3 minutes. Add the tomato paste and thyme and cook another minute, stirring frequently. Add the broth, puréed corn, bay leaf, 1 teaspoon salt, and pepper to taste.

05 While bringing the chowder to a boil, peel the potato, cut it into 1/2-inch dice, and add it to the pot. Cover the pot and simmer until the potato is tender, 25 to 35 minutes.

06 Remove the bay leaf. Add the reserved corn kernels, roasted sweet potatoes, and parsley. Thin with soymilk, if necessary. Adjust seasonings. Cook (but do not boil after adding soymilk) until heated throughout.

CHAPTER FIVE

THE **MAIN COURSE**

Layer tortillas with a colorful roasted corn and black bean salad to create a stack. Top it with a dollop of rich Silken Cilantro Sauce for a very pretty dish—good for a festive lunch or supper.

Since the tortillas are crisped in the oven, they crack rather than slice. Encourage your guests to use their hands to lift a chip of tortilla with some of the topping when a fork isn't practical.

CRISP TORTILLA STACKS WITH ROASTED
CORN AND BLACK BEANS

01 Set the broiler rack about 5 inches from the element and preheat the broiler. Spread out the corn, jalapeños, and green bell pepper on a large, nonstick roasting or baking pan. Drizzle with 1 tablespoon of the olive oil, and sprinkle with salt and pepper. Broil for 3 minutes, stir, and then continue broiling until some of the corn kernels are speckled with brown spots, 3 to 5 minutes longer. Transfer the vegetables to a large bowl.

02 Spread out the tomatoes and red onion on the same pan. Drizzle with the remaining tablespoon of oil. Season well with salt and pepper. Broil for 4 minutes, toss, and then continue to broil until the onions or tomatoes begin to be tinged around the edges, 3 to 5 minutes longer. Add to the bowl along with the black beans and cilantro. Add enough salt, pepper, and lime juice to give the mixture lots of flavor.

03 Turn off the broiler. Set a shelf in the middle of the oven and set the temperature to 400°F. Just before you are ready to serve, set the tortillas directly on the oven rack and toast until crisp, 3 to 4 minutes. (Or, if you prefer, heat the tortillas just until they are warm, but still pliable.)

04 To assemble each stack, set a tortilla on a large dinner plate and mound about $3/4$ cup of roasted corn salad on top. Cover with a second tortilla and another $3/4$ cup of corn salad. Spoon a heaping tablespoon of Silken Cilantro Sauce on top. Place 2 lime wedges on either side of the plate. Serve warm or at room temperature. Pass the extra Cilantro Sauce in a bowl.

3 CUPS FRESH OR FROZEN CORN KERNELS

1 OR 2 JALAPEÑOS, SEEDED AND FINELY DICED

1 LARGE GREEN BELL PEPPER, SEEDED AND DICED

2 TABLESPOONS OLIVE OIL

SALT AND FRESHLY GROUND PEPPER

1 POUND PLUM TOMATOES, COARSELY CHOPPED

2 CUPS DICED RED ONION

ABOUT 1 $3/4$ CUPS COOKED BLACK BEANS OR ONE 15-OUNCE CAN, DRAINED AND RINSED

$1/2$ CUP CHOPPED CILANTRO

4 TO 5 TABLESPOONS FRESHLY SQUEEZED LIME JUICE

8 CORN TORTILLAS (ABOUT 6 INCHES IN DIAMETER)

SILKEN CILANTRO SAUCE (PAGE 93)

2 LIMES, CUT INTO WEDGES

2 TO 3 TABLESPOONS OLIVE OIL

12 OUNCES CREMINI OR BUTTON MUSHROOMS, TRIMMED AND SLICED

SALT

1 ½ CUPS THINLY SLICED LEEKS

2 TEASPOONS MINCED GARLIC

2 TEASPOONS DRIED HERBES DE PROVENCE (PAGE 14) OR ½ TEA-SPOON EACH DRIED TARRAGON, THYME OR MARJORAM, BASIL, AND ROSEMARY (BREAK INTO TINY PIECES)

1 TEASPOON FENNEL SEEDS

½ CUP DRY WHITE WINE OR VERMOUTH

4 CUPS VEGETABLE BROTH

1 CUP FRENCH GREEN LENTILS

2 CUPS DICED FENNEL OR CELERY

TWO 9-OUNCE PACKAGES FROZEN ARTICHOKE HEARTS

½ CUP PICHOLINE OR NIÇOISE OLIVES OR OTHER SMALL MEDITERRANEAN BRINE-CURED OLIVES (OR A COMBINATION)

2 TEASPOONS GRATED LEMON ZEST

2 TO 3 TEASPOONS BALSAMIC SYRUP (PAGE 16)

PARSLEY AIOLI (RECIPE OPPOSITE)

CHOPPED FENNEL FRONDS, FOR GARNISH (OPTIONAL)

The small, speckled green legumes known as Le Puy lentils have a fine taste and can be counted on to hold their shape. Usually labeled French lentils, they are sold in gourmet shops and some health-food stores.

In this soupy stew, I've used the lentils as a backdrop for ingredients common to the south of France: artichoke hearts, mushrooms, black niçoise and green picholine olives, and the garlicky mayonnaise known as aioli. Warn your guests to be on the lookout for olive pits, which are tedious to remove.

The Parsley Aioli gives this wintry dish a bright finish. The aioli also makes a nice spread for slices of baguette—an ideal accompaniment to the stew, as is an arugula and endive salad. For an even heartier meal, set a wedge of Potato Cake (page 85) alongside each portion.

PROVENÇAL GREEN LENTILS WITH ARTICHOKES, MUSHROOMS, AND PARSLEY AIOLI

01 Heat 1 tablespoon of the oil in a heavy 5- to 6-quart, nonreactive pot. Add the mushrooms and immediately sprinkle them with ½ tea-spoon salt. Cook over medium-high heat, stirring almost constantly, until the mushrooms are nicely browned, 4 to 5 minutes. Add more oil during this time if the mushrooms begin to stick.

02 Add another tablespoon of oil, the leeks, garlic, herbs, and fennel seeds. Cook over medium-high heat, stirring frequently, until the leeks soften slightly, 2 to 3 minutes. Add the wine and cook until most of it evaporates, about 1 minute.

03 Add the broth, lentils, and fennel and bring to a boil. Cover and cook at a gentle boil until the lentils are tender, 40 to 50 minutes. About halfway through, taste the stew and add more herbs if you think they're needed.

04 Set the artichoke hearts in a colander and run them under hot water to break up the blocks and wash away any ice crystals. Stir the artichoke hearts and olives into the lentils. Cover and cook until the artichoke hearts are tender, 3 to 4 minutes.

05 Add salt to taste, lemon zest, and enough Balsamic Syrup to round out the flavors. Serve in shallow soup bowls, topped with Parsley Aioli. Garnish with fennel fronds, if available, and pass any extra aioli in a bowl.

PARSLEY AIOLI

01 Put the lemon juice and oil in a blender jar, and then add the remaining ingredients. Process until very smooth, about 2 minutes, scraping down the sides of the jar once or twice. Add more lemon juice and salt, if needed, to balance the flavors.

02 Use immediately or refrigerate in a tightly sealed container for up to 3 days. (The color is likely to turn olive, but the flavor will be fine.) Thin leftovers, if necessary, with a little water.

OTHER IDEAS

Use mixed wild mushrooms instead of cremini.

Omit the Parsley Aioli and stir in fresh thyme leaves just before serving.

Leftover aioli makes a good topping for baked potato or a dip for raw vegetables. It also makes a fine mayonnaise-like sandwich spread.

MAKES ¾ CUP

2 TABLESPOONS LEMON JUICE, PLUS MORE IF NEEDED

2 TABLESPOONS OLIVE OIL

2 CUPS TIGHTLY PACKED PARSLEY LEAVES AND TENDER STEMS

4 OUNCES (½ CUP) SILKEN SOFT OR FIRM TOFU

10 LARGE CLOVES ROASTED GARLIC (PAGE 12), PEELED

½ TEASPOON DIJON MUSTARD

½ TEASPOON SALT, PLUS MORE IF NEEDED

1 POUND OR TWO 10-OUNCE PINTS BRUSSELS SPROUTS

2 TEASPOONS OLIVE OIL

1 TABLESPOON PEELED, MINCED GINGER

1/2 TEASPOON MINCED GARLIC

6 SCALLIONS, THINLY SLICED (KEEP WHITE AND GREEN PARTS SEPARATE)

1/2 CUP FINELY DICED RED BELL PEPPERS

1/2 CUP FINELY DICED YELLOW OR PURPLE BELL PEPPERS, OR ADDITIONAL RED PEPPERS

1/4 TO 1/2 TEASPOON CRUSHED RED PEPPER FLAKES

3/4 CUP WATER

8 OUNCES UDON NOODLES (EDEN FOODS MAKES A NICE BROWN RICE UDON)

2 1/2 TABLESPOONS DARK MISO

1 TABLESPOON ROSEMARY-INFUSED OLIVE OIL (OR 1 TABLESPOON OLIVE OIL AND 1 TO 2 TEASPOONS CHOPPED FRESH ROSEMARY), PLUS MORE IF NEEDED

1 TO 2 TABLESPOONS JAPANESE SOY SAUCE (SHOYU OR TAMARI)

1/2 CUP TOASTED PECANS

If you've never sliced Brussels sprouts before tossing them into the pot, you're about to discover the ideal way to prepare this underappreciated vegetable. Since the slices cook evenly and maintain their sprightly green color and crunch, you will feel like you are being introduced to a new vegetable.

In this dish, you'll be tossing the sliced Brussels sprouts with Japanese udon noodles, bell peppers, and pecans. An East-West sauce is quickly made by blending the fermented soybean paste called miso with rosemary-infused olive oil and a little of the noodle cooking-water. This recipe calls for dark miso (page 15), which is generally saltier and aged longer than light miso, so avoid any temptation to make a substitution. You'll find udon noodles and miso in Asian groceries and health-food stores. Leftovers are likely to need perking up with soy sauce or lemon juice.

BRUSSELS SPROUTS AND UDON NOODLES IN MISO SAUCE

01 Trim off the root end of the Brussels sprouts, and discard any browned or damaged outer leaves. Cut the Brussels sprouts lengthwise into 1/4-inch slices. Set aside. Begin bringing a large pot of water to the boil for the udon.

02 In a large skillet, heat the oil. Add the ginger and garlic, and cook over medium-high heat, stirring constantly, for about 20 seconds. Add the sliced white part of the scallions, bell peppers, and red pepper flakes and cook, stirring frequently, for 1 minute.

03 Turn off the heat. Standing back to avoid spattering oil, add the water. Add the Brussels sprouts, cover, and cook over medium-high heat until the sprouts are tender-crisp and still bright green, 2 to 4 minutes. (Add a few tablespoons additional water during this time if the mixture becomes dry.) Set the skillet aside, uncovered.

04 Break the udon in half and add them to the boiling water. In a small bowl, dissolve the miso in 1/2 cup of the noodle cooking-water. Stir in the rosemary-infused oil and 1 tablespoon of soy sauce.

05 When the noodles are just short of done, drain them. Set them in the skillet with the Brussels sprouts, and stir in the miso sauce and reserved scallion greens. Add more soy sauce and rosemary oil, if needed. Cook over medium heat, stirring constantly, just until the mixture is good and hot. Toss in the pecans and serve immediately.

CURRIED TEMPEH

8 OUNCES TEMPEH (SOY OR THREE-GRAIN)

2 TABLESPOONS MILD CURRY POWDER, SUCH AS THE ONE MADE BY MERWANJEE POONJIANJEE & SONS

1/2 TEASPOON GROUND TURMERIC

PINCH OF SALT

1 1/2 TABLESPOONS GRATED FRESH GINGER (SEE PAGE 13)

2 TABLESPOONS PEANUT OIL

1/3 CUP WATER

SKILLET GRAIN MEDLEY

1 CUP WATER, PLUS MORE IF NEEDED

1/2 CUP GRATED, DRIED, UNSWEETENED COCONUT (AVAILABLE IN HEALTH-FOOD STORES)

1 TEASPOON FENNEL SEEDS

1 TEASPOON CUMIN SEEDS

1/4 TEASPOON SALT, PLUS MORE IF NEEDED

1/4 TEASPOON GROUND CINNAMON

1/8 TEASPOON CAYENNE (OPTIONAL)

3 CUPS COOKED GRAINS (SEE PAGE 21; IF FROZEN, POUR BOILING WATER OVER THEM TO PARTIALLY DEFROST)

1/2 CUP FROZEN GREEN PEAS

CUCUMBER-MINT "RAITA" (PAGE 92)

Season tempeh cubes with a curry marinade, and then mound these exotic "croutons" on top of Indian-spiced grains. You can use whatever cooked grains you have on hand, but the texture is more interesting when you use two or three different types.

Make this dish only if you have time to prepare the Cucumber-Mint "Raita" as well, since a soupy accompaniment is needed to moisten the grains and offer a smooth contrast to their chewiness. A side dish of Carrot Slaw with Mango Chutney Dressing (page 90) adds a welcome crunch. Offer a bowl of Patak's Brinjal Eggplant Relish (this is really good!) for those who would enjoy a hit of intense flavor. (You can find Patak's products in Indian groceries and many supermarkets.)

Microwave any leftovers in a bowl lightly covered with a paper towel or waxed paper. If the grains are quite dried out, sprinkle them with a little water before reheating.

SKILLET **GRAIN** MEDLEY WITH CURRIED **TEMPEH**

01 Set the rack in the middle of the oven and preheat the oven to 425°F.

02 To prepare the curried tempeh: Use a fork to prick both sides of the tempeh deeply about 20 times. Cut the slab into 1/2-inch cubes and set aside.

03 In a sealable storage container, combine the curry powder, turmeric, salt, grated ginger, oil, and water. Add the tempeh cubes, close the container, and shake gently to coat the cubes evenly. (Most of the marinade will be absorbed instantly.) Set aside for 5 minutes.

04 Arrange the tempeh in one layer in a nonstick baking pan or shallow roasting pan. (Set aside the storage container and any unabsorbed marinade.) Bake the tempeh for 5 minutes. Toss, and then continue to bake until the cubes feel crisp and dry to the touch, 5 to 7 minutes longer. (Do not bake longer than 12 minutes, as the tempeh will dry out; it may not brown significantly.) Set aside in a warm place.

05 To prepare the grain medley: Pour the water into the container you used for the tempeh marinade, and blend in any unabsorbed marinade. Heat a large, nonstick skillet and add the coconut, fennel seeds, and cumin seeds. Stir almost constantly until the coconut becomes fragrant and about half of the batch turns golden, 1 to 2 minutes. (Take care as the coconut can burn quickly.)

06 Immediately pour the marinade water into the pan and stir. Add the salt, cinnamon, and cayenne (if using). Boil gently for 2 minutes. Stir in the grains, peas, and more salt, if needed. Cover and cook over medium-low heat until good and hot, stirring occasionally to prevent the grains from sticking, 2 to 3 minutes. Stir in a few table-spoons more water during this time if the mixture becomes dry.

07 To serve: Mound the grains in the center of large lipped plates or shallow soup bowls. Surround with "moats" of Cucumber-Mint "Raita," and top with the Curried Tempeh.

OTHER IDEAS

Prepare the Curried Tempeh on its own and stuff cubes into pita with shredded lettuce or chopped, steamed vegetables. Use the "Raita" as a dressing.

Crumble any leftover Curried Tempeh on top of a green salad or steamed vegetables.

Jade-green broccoli vies with red and yellow bell peppers for center stage in this exotic Asian stew. For relatively little effort, this recipe rewards you with a sophisticated sauce reminiscent of Thai restaurant fare.

The only ingredient you may not recognize here is seitan, a dense, high-protein meat substitute made of wheat gluten. Seitan plays a big role in the Buddhist vegetarian kitchen and is traditionally seasoned with soy sauce (and sometimes ginger); its flavor contributes nicely to the sauce.

You'll find seitan in the refrigerated section of health-food stores. Don't be discouraged when you open the plastic tub and discover large, strange-looking chunks. Once chopped finely, the seitan adds real substance and a delightfully chewy texture.

Lime juice is needed to balance the sauce, but it quickly dulls the sprightly color, so serve wedges of lime on the side and let everyone squeeze to taste. I like to serve this dish in large, shallow soup bowls over Thai jasmine or basmati rice.

THAI-INSPIRED BROCCOLI IN COCONUT-CILANTRO SAUCE

01 Cut the broccoli florets from the stalks, and separate them into small pieces. Trim the stalks, and use a paring knife or peeler to remove the fibrous outer layers. Cut the stalks into 1/2-inch chunks. Set the florets and stalks aside.

02 With the motor of the food processor running, pop the garlic and then the ginger, shallot, and jalapeño(s) into the feed tube, and chop finely. Reserve 1/2 cup tightly packed cilantro leaves. Chop the remaining cilantro a few times, add to the processor, and chop finely. Add the coconut milk, sugar, and salt, and process to blend thoroughly.

03 Transfer the coconut milk mixture to a 4- or 5-quart pot, and bring to a boil. Boil gently, uncovered, stirring occasionally, for 3 minutes.

04 Meanwhile, remove the seitan from its tub. Reserve any marinating liquid if you like its taste, and add enough water to equal a total of 1 cup liquid. Stir this liquid (or 1 cup plain water) into the coconut milk mixture. Chop the seitan finely in the processor, and add it to the pot along with the reserved broccoli.

CONTINUED

SERVES **4**

2 POUNDS BROCCOLI (3 LARGE STALKS)

1 LARGE CLOVE GARLIC

1-INCH CHUNK GINGER, TRIMMED AND CUT INTO EIGHTHS (PEELING IS NOT NECESSARY)

1 MEDIUM SHALLOT (ABOUT 2 OUNCES), PEELED AND QUARTERED

1 OR 2 JALAPEÑOS (DEPENDING UPON DESIRED HEAT), HALVED AND SEEDED

1 GOOD-SIZED BUNCH CILANTRO (ABOUT 4 OUNCES; INCLUDE STEMS AND ROOTS, IF AVAILABLE, BUT RINSE THOROUGHLY TO REMOVE ALL SAND)

ONE 13.5-OUNCE CAN COCONUT MILK (NOT LIGHT)

1 1/2 TEASPOONS SUGAR

1/2 TEASPOON SALT

8 TO 12 OUNCES SEITAN (WHEAT GLUTEN)

1 LARGE RED BELL PEPPER, SEEDED AND CUT INTO 1/4-INCH STRIPS

1 LARGE YELLOW BELL PEPPER, SEEDED AND CUT INTO 1/4-INCH STRIPS

1 TO 3 TABLESPOONS JAPANESE SOY SAUCE (TAMARI OR SHOYU)

A FEW BASIL LEAVES, SHREDDED, FOR GARNISH (OPTIONAL)

2 LIMES, CUT INTO WEDGES

05 Cover and cook at a moderate boil for 2 minutes. Add the bell peppers, cover, and continue cooking, stirring once or twice, until the broccoli is tender but still bright green, 3 to 4 minutes longer. Add more water during this time if the mixture becomes dry.

06 Just before serving, coarsely chop the reserved cilantro leaves and stir them in. Add enough soy sauce to create a good balance of flavors. Ladle into soup bowls, and garnish with basil, if you wish. Accompany each portion with a few lime wedges.

OTHER IDEAS

Toss with cooked rice noodles. Season with additional soy sauce and garnish with chopped roasted peanuts and bean sprouts.

Substitute Smart Ground for the seitan. Smart Ground, crumbles made of soy protein concentrate and wheat gluten, is available in health-food stores and some supermarkets.

Here's the game plan for preparing this wintry casserole. While cooking brown rice in a rich, herb-scented porcini broth on top of the stove, you'll be roasting root vegetables in the oven. Scatter the vegetables over the moist grains and season with a drizzle of sweet-puckery balsamic syrup, which brings this dish over the top. It's a colorful medley, full of contrasting tastes and textures.

I love the chewiness of short-grain brown rice—it's so much more interesting than the long-grain variety. Toss in some black buffalo barley or Colusari red rice to add visual interest. You don't have to worry about exact quantities of vegetables for roasting: a little more or less doesn't matter.

This casserole may seem a bit soupy at first, but any extra liquid will disappear quickly as the thirsty grains drink it up.

PORCINI BROWN RICE WITH ROASTED ROOT VEGETABLES AND BALSAMIC SYRUP

SERVES **4 TO 6**

1 OUNCE PORCINI OR OTHER DRIED MUSHROOMS (ABOUT ¾ CUP LOOSELY PACKED)

4 CUPS BOILING WATER

1 POUND RED-SKINNED POTATOES, TRIMMED AND CUT INTO 1-INCH CHUNKS

½ POUND BABY-CUT CARROTS

½ POUND PARSNIPS, PEELED AND CUT INTO ½-INCH CHUNKS

3 MEDIUM RED ONIONS (ABOUT 1 POUND), PEELED AND QUARTERED

3 TABLESPOONS OLIVE OIL, DIVIDED

1 TO 2 TEASPOONS DRIED ROSEMARY (BROKEN INTO BITS), THYME, OR MARJORAM

SALT AND FRESHLY GROUND PEPPER

2 CUPS CHOPPED LEEKS OR ONIONS

1 CUP DICED FENNEL OR CELERY

2 TEASPOONS ITALIAN HERB BLEND (PAGE 14 OR STORE-BOUGHT)

1 CUP SHORT-GRAIN BROWN RICE

½ CUP BLACK BUFFALO BARLEY, COLUSARI RED RICE, OR ADDITIONAL BROWN RICE

1 BAY LEAF

3 TABLESPOONS MINCED PARSLEY, FOR GARNISH (OPTIONAL)

BALSAMIC SYRUP (PAGE 16)

01 Set the porcini in a bowl and pour the boiling water on top. Cover and set aside for 10 minutes or longer.

02 Arrange the potatoes, carrots, parsnips, and red onions in one layer in one or two roasting pans. Drizzle with 2 tablespoons of the olive oil. Sprinkle with the rosemary, and season well with salt and pepper. Set two racks in the middle portion of the oven, and start preheating the oven to 450°F. Set the vegetables aside while you turn your attention to the rice.

03 Lift the porcini from the soaking liquid with a slotted spoon, and coarsely chop any large pieces. Set the porcini and soaking liquid aside.

04 Heat a tablespoon of oil in a heavy 3-quart pot over medium-high heat. Cook the leeks and fennel for 3 minutes, stirring frequently. Stir in the Italian herbs and cook for another few seconds. Pour in the reserved porcini liquid, taking care to leave any grit behind. Add the porcini, grains, bay leaf, and 1¼ teaspoons salt. Bring to a boil, reduce the heat, cover, and cook over low heat until the grains are tender, about 40 minutes. (Some broth may not be absorbed.)

CONTINUED

05 While the grains are cooking, roast the vegetables, tossing every 10 or 15 minutes, until tender and easily pierced with the tip of a paring knife, 30 to 40 minutes in all. (A few tips: Rotate the roasting pan(s) if the vegetables are browning unevenly. The onions are done when lightly singed around the edges; they'll remain slightly crunchy. Remove any vegetables that begin to burn or dry out before the others are done.)

06 When the grains are ready (they will remain slightly chewy, even when fully cooked), remove the bay leaf and add more salt, if needed. Cover and let sit off the heat for 5 minutes, or until the roasted vegetables are ready.

07 To serve, reheat the roasted vegetables, if necessary. Mound the grains on individual plates. Spoon any unabsorbed porcini broth over the grains. Distribute the vegetables on top or alongside. Sprinkle with parsley, if you wish, and drizzle 1 to 2 teaspoons of Balsamic Syrup over each portion.

OTHER IDEAS

KAMUT AND WILD RICE VARIATION

Substitute kamut for the brown rice and wild rice for the black buffalo barley. Soak the kamut and wild rice overnight, then drain and proceed as directed. The grains may need as long as 50 minutes to cook, and the mixture will be somewhat soupy.

Instead of rice and barley, use a colorful grain mix, such as the one sold under the Lundberg label.

Substitute fresh herbs for the dried, using double the amount.

In my version of this zesty Cuban lunch-counter favorite, finely chopped wheat gluten (usually sold under its Japanese name, seitan; see page 51) makes an admirable substitute for the traditional ground beef. Sweet raisins, salty olives, and pickled capers infuse the tomato sauce and seitan with irresistible flavor. For optimum taste, prepare the picadillo a few hours before serving, or even the day before.

Opt for chicken-style seitan if you can find it, as the taste is more appropriate to this dish. Traditionally seasoned seitan, typically flavored with soy sauce and ginger, can be used successfully in the picadillo if you rinse away most of the seasoning, as directed in the recipe. Serve the picadillo over quinoa or rice tossed with toasted pumpkin seeds or with Savory Grains (page 84).

A CUBAN PICADILLO

12 TO 16 OUNCES SEITAN (WHEAT GLUTEN), PREFERABLY CHICKEN STYLE, DRAINED

1 TABLESPOON OLIVE OIL

1 TABLESPOON CHOPPED GARLIC

1 CUP CHOPPED ONION

2 MEDIUM GREEN PEPPERS, SEEDED AND DICED

1 TEASPOON DRIED OREGANO LEAVES

1/4 TEASPOON GROUND CUMIN

2 CUPS UNSEASONED TOMATO JUICE

ONE 15-OUNCE CAN DICED TOMATOES WITH GREEN CHILES, WITH LIQUID

1/3 CUP PIMENTO-STUFFED GREEN OLIVES, CUT INTO THIRDS CROSS-WISE

1/4 CUP RAISINS

2 TABLESPOONS DRAINED CAPERS

1/2 TEASPOON SALT

FRESHLY GROUND BLACK PEPPER

01 Place the seitan in the bowl of a food processor and pulse until it is chopped to a texture resembling ground meat. (Or chop finely by hand.) If using the traditionally seasoned variety, soak the chopped seitan in water to cover for 10 minutes. Drain. Taste and repeat with fresh water, if necessary, until the seitan tastes fairly bland. Drain thoroughly and set aside.

02 Heat the oil in a large saucepan over medium-high heat. Add the garlic and cook, stirring frequently, until it is lightly browned, about 30 seconds. Immediately stir in the onion and green peppers and cook over medium heat, stirring occasionally, until the vegetables have softened somewhat, 4 to 5 minutes. Stir in the oregano and cumin and cook for about 30 seconds. Then add the reserved chopped seitan and the remaining ingredients.

03 Bring to a boil over high heat, reduce the heat, and cook uncovered at a gentle boil, stirring occasionally, until the mixture has thickened slightly and the seitan has picked up the flavor of the sauce, 30 to 45 minutes. Adjust seasonings before serving.

OTHER IDEAS

Substitute Smart Ground for the seitan. Smart Ground, crumbles made of soy protein concentrate and wheat gluten, is available in health-food stores and some supermarkets.

There's something delightful and festive about stuffed vegetables. In this case, each diner gets an impressive eggplant "barge" bearing a cargo of curried chickpeas. Unlike most stuffed vegetable dishes, this one is quick and easy to prepare.

You'll start by roasting halved eggplants, then scooping out the flesh and cooking it with chickpeas, tomatoes, dried coconut, and toasted mustard seeds. You can make this filling as hot as you like by adding cayenne. Since cayenne is potent stuff, start with a pinch and add more gradually. To speed things up, begin preparing the ingredients for the filling while the eggplant is in the oven.

Carrot Slaw with Mango Chutney Dressing (page 90) makes a nice accompaniment. The stuffed eggplant is quite filling, so most people will do just fine without rice.

TOMATO-CHICKPEA CURRY IN EGGPLANT SHELLS

2 MEDIUM EGGPLANTS (1 TO 1 1/4 POUNDS EACH)

2 TO 3 TABLESPOONS VEGETABLE OIL, DIVIDED

SALT TO TASTE, PLUS 1/4 TEASPOON

FRESHLY GROUND PEPPER

2 TABLESPOONS BROWN MUSTARD SEEDS (THEY'RE ACTUALLY REDDISH BROWN)

2 CUPS COARSELY CHOPPED ONIONS

1 1/2 TABLESPOONS MILD CURRY POWDER, SUCH AS MERWANJEE POONJIANJEE & SONS, PLUS MORE IF NEEDED

ONE 15-OUNCE CAN DICED TOMATOES, WITH LIQUID

1 1/2 CUPS COOKED CHICKPEAS OR ONE 15-OUNCE CAN, DRAINED

1/2 CUP DRIED, UNSWEETENED, GRATED COCONUT (AVAILABLE IN HEALTH-FOOD STORES)

CAYENNE

CHOPPED CILANTRO, FOR GARNISH (OPTIONAL)

01 Set the rack in the middle of the oven and preheat to 450°F. Lightly oil one or two roasting pans large enough to hold the eggplant halves in one layer. Add 1/8 inch of water.

02 Leaving the stem intact, halve the eggplants lengthwise. Use the tip of a paring knife to score the flesh side deeply in a crisscross pattern. Brush the cut side with oil, season with salt and pepper, and set flesh side down in the roasting pans. Brush the skins with oil.

03 Roast until the eggplants are tender and easily pierced with the tip of a paring knife, 18 to 25 minutes. (Check after 10 minutes and add more water, if needed.) When the eggplants are cool enough to handle, use a paring or grapefruit knife to create a 1/2-inch "wall" all around, and then scoop out the flesh. Coarsely chop the flesh (including seeds) and set aside. Lightly season the eggplant shells with salt and pepper, and reserve them in a warm place.

04 To prepare the filling, first toast the mustard seeds: Heat 1 tablespoon of oil in a large, heavy saucepan over high heat. Stir in the mustard seeds, cover the pot, and leave the heat turned to high. Listen carefully: as soon as you hear the mustard seeds begin to pop against the lid, turn off the heat (remove to a cool burner if using an electric stove), and wait for the popping to subside. Most of the seeds should now be gray.

CONTINUED

05 Stir the onions into the mustard seeds and cook over medium-high heat, stirring frequently, until the onions start to brown, 4 to 5 minutes. Add a bit more oil during this time if the onions are sticking. Stir in the curry powder and cook for 10 seconds. Then add the tomatoes, chickpeas, coconut, reserved eggplant flesh, salt, and cayenne to taste. Cover and simmer over medium heat, stirring occasionally, until the chickpeas develop a curried flavor, about 15 minutes. During this time, add more curry and salt, if needed, and stir in a few tablespoons of water if the mixture becomes dry.

06 Mound the filling into the eggplant shells. (If you have a little extra filling, enjoy a snack.) Garnish with a sprinkling of cilantro, if you wish, and serve immediately.

OTHER IDEAS

If you're not fond of coconut, feel free to leave it out. (You may need less salt.)

Substitute diced tomatoes with green chiles for the plain tomatoes.

This combination was inspired by the popular street food of Trinidad and Jamaica. In my version, chunks of tempeh are quickly marinated with typical jerk spices and then baked. The dense, zesty cubes are dotted on top of meltingly soft, curried calabaza—a large West Indian pumpkin that is sold in wedges in many Hispanic markets. (You can substitute butternut squash.) The combination is quite filling, so you probably won't need a grain accompaniment.

I've organized the recipe for maximum efficiency, so you'll be preparing the curried pumpkin while the tempeh is marinating. If it's more convenient, you can marinate the tempeh overnight.

WEST INDIAN **PUMPKIN** WITH JERK-SPICED **TEMPEH**

01 With a fork, deeply prick the tempeh about 20 times on each side. Cut into 1/2-inch dice. Set aside.

02 In a blender, combine the soy sauce, oil, brown sugar, garlic, ginger, thyme, allspice, pepper, salt, and onion. Purée until very smooth, about 1 minute. Add hot sauce to taste. Reserve 1/4 cup of the marinade.

03 Pour half of the remaining marinade into a storage container. Add the diced tempeh. Pour the rest of the marinade on top. Cover, then shake gently to coat the tempeh evenly. Set aside for 15 minutes (or refrigerate overnight).

04 While the tempeh is marinating, prepare the curried pumpkin: Heat the oil in a large, heavy saucepan. Cook the onion and green pepper over medium heat, stirring frequently, until softened, 4 to 5 minutes. Stir in the tomatoes, 1/2 cup tomato juice, 3 tablespoons of the reserved tempeh marinade, and the smaller amounts of curry, cinnamon, cloves, and salt. Stir in the pumpkin. Cover and simmer, stirring occasionally, until the pumpkin is tender, 20 to 25 minutes. During this time, adjust the seasoning by adding more marinade and spices if you wish. Add more tomato juice or water if the sauce becomes too thick.

05 While the pumpkin is cooking, preheat the oven to 425°F. Brush a large nonstick baking sheet or roasting pan with oil (if not nonstick,

CONTINUED

SERVES **6**

JERK-SPICED TEMPEH

8 OUNCES TEMPEH (SOY OR THREE-GRAIN)

3 TABLESPOONS JAPANESE SOY SAUCE (SHOYU OR TAMARI)

2 TABLESPOONS VEGETABLE OIL, PLUS OIL FOR PREPARING THE PAN

1/4 CUP DARK BROWN SUGAR

2 LARGE CLOVES GARLIC, PEELED AND QUARTERED

1 TEASPOON GROUND GINGER

3/4 TO 1 TEASPOON DRIED THYME LEAVES

1/2 TEASPOON GROUND ALLSPICE

1/4 TEASPOON FRESHLY GROUND BLACK PEPPER

1/4 TEASPOON SALT

1 MEDIUM VIDALIA, WALLA WALLA, OR OTHER SWEET ONION (ABOUT 6 OUNCES), PEELED AND CUT INTO EIGHTHS

PICKAPEPPA, TABASCO, OR OTHER HOT SAUCE

WEST INDIAN PUMPKIN

1 TABLESPOON VEGETABLE OIL

1 CUP CHOPPED ONION

1 LARGE GREEN BELL PEPPER, SEEDED AND DICED

ONE 15-OUNCE CAN DICED TOMATOES (WITH LIQUID)

½ TO 1 CUP UNSEASONED TOMATO JUICE OR WATER

3 TO 4 TABLESPOONS MARINADE (RESERVED FROM JERK-SPICED TEMPEH)

1 TO 2 TEASPOONS CURRY POWDER

¼ TEASPOON GROUND CINNAMON

⅛ TO ¼ TEASPOON GROUND CLOVES

½ TEASPOON SALT

2 ½ POUNDS CARIBBEAN PUMPKIN (CALABAZA) OR BUTTERNUT SQUASH, PEELED AND CUT INTO ¾-INCH CUBES

line with oiled foil). Spread the marinated tempeh in the pan in one layer. (It's okay if some of the unabsorbed marinade ends up in the pan.) Bake until the color deepens and the top of each piece feels fairly dry and is no longer sticky to the touch, 10 to 12 minutes. (Do not cook the tempeh longer than 12 minutes, as it will dry out.)

06 To serve, spoon the curried pumpkin onto dinner plates and set the jerk-spiced tempeh on top.

OTHER IDEAS

Instead of using hot sauce, flavor the tempeh marinade with ¼ to 1 teaspoon chipotle in adobo, a condiment made of smoked jalapeños in a seasoned tomato sauce (available in Hispanic groceries and gourmet shops).

WEST INDIAN "ROTI" WRAPS

Place chunks of pumpkin and tempeh just below the center of a large flour tortilla. Fold the bottom of the tortilla over the filling. Fold over the sides and then the top to create a packet. Reheat in the microwave if necessary. It's best to serve these on plates with knives and forks, as they're messy to eat.

WEST INDIAN "PIZZA"

Place a warm flour tortilla on each plate and spoon the pumpkin and tempeh on top.

This nourishing winter casserole takes only a few minutes to assemble but a few hours to bake. The recipe is based on the principle of slow-cooking unsoaked beans for a few hours in a 250°F oven (see page 18). The beans develop a creamy texture, and the mountain of escarole melts into the olive-infused broth, creating a voluptuous environment. For optimum flavor, try to locate cannellini, which are available in Italian markets and gourmet shops; they have better flavor and texture than Great Northern beans.

To give this mellow dish a bright finish, dot the top with a sprinkling of vibrant gremolata, the classic Italian condiment made of finely chopped parsley, lemon peel, and garlic.

While the casserole is in the oven, consider making Slow-Roasted Tomatoes and Fennel (page 80) on the rack below. Serve them on the side.

SLOW-BAKED **CANNELLINI** WITH **OLIVES, ESCAROLE,** AND **GREMOLATA**

2 TABLESPOONS OLIVE OIL

8 OUNCES CREMINI OR BUTTON MUSHROOMS, TRIMMED AND SLICED

1/2 TEASPOON SALT

2 CUPS THINLY SLICED LEEKS

2 LARGE CLOVES GARLIC, THINLY SLICED

1 1/2 TEASPOONS DRIED ROSEMARY (CRUMBLED INTO BITS) OR ITALIAN HERB BLEND (PAGE 14)

4 CUPS VEGETABLE BROTH (USE HALF WATER IF BROTH IS SALTED)

1/2 CUP OIL-CURED BLACK OLIVES (PITTING OPTIONAL)

1 1/2 TO 2 POUNDS ESCAROLE, COARSELY CHOPPED

1 CUP DRIED CANNELLINI OR GREAT NORTHERN BEANS, PICKED OVER AND RINSED

FRESHLY GROUND PEPPER

BALSAMIC SYRUP (PAGE 16) OR GOOD-QUALITY BALSAMIC VINEGAR TO TASTE

GREMOLATA

1 MEDIUM LEMON

1 CUP TIGHTLY PACKED PARSLEY LEAVES

1 CLOVE GARLIC (SMALL OR LARGE, DEPENDING ON HOW MUCH YOU LOVE IT), THINLY SLICED

01 Set the rack in the middle of the oven. (If slow-roasting fennel and tomatoes, set the second rack a few inches below.) Preheat the oven to 250°F.

02 Heat the oil in a heavy, 6-quart stove-to-oven casserole or Dutch oven. Cook the mushrooms over medium-high heat, stirring frequently, for 1 minute. Sprinkle with the salt (this will force the mushrooms to give up some liquid), and continue cooking and stirring until the mushrooms are browned and tender, 3 to 4 minutes longer.

03 Toss in the leeks, garlic, and rosemary, and cook over medium-high heat, stirring frequently, until the leeks have wilted, about 3 minutes. Add the broth and olives and bring to a boil. Add half of the escarole, cover, and cook until it wilts, about 1 minute. Stir well. Add the remaining escarole and repeat.

04 Turn off the heat. Push the vegetables aside and add the beans, taking care that they are buried under the escarole and covered with liquid. Cover, transfer the casserole to the oven, and bake until the beans are tender, 1 1/2 to 3 hours. Toward the end of cooking,

CONTINUED

add salt if needed and pepper to taste. (The stew may seem soupy at first, but will quickly thicken as it stands.)

05 Just before serving, prepare the gremolata: Use a standard swivel vegetable peeler with very gentle pressure to remove the lemon zest (the yellow part only) in strips. (I find this works best when I move the peeler back and forth as I'm moving it down.) Place the strips on a chopping board with the parsley and garlic and finely chop them together. Cut 4 thin slices of the lemon to use as garnish.

06 To serve, stir in enough Balsamic Syrup to sharpen the flavors. Ladle the stew into large, shallow soup bowls. (Pasta bowls work well.) Float the lemon slices in the middle, and sprinkle a generous amount of gremolata on top.

OTHER IDEAS

Add finely chopped fennel stalks when you add the beans. Include chopped fennel fronds in the gremolata.

Substitute large lima beans for the cannellini. They will expand to the size of small potatoes.

Here's my favorite way to prepare roasted portobello caps: Brush them with a mixture of olive oil, soy sauce, and balsamic vinegar and pop them into the oven. Although you won't taste the soy sauce, it turns the caps a deep burnished brown and enhances the mushrooms' flavor.

Serve the portobellos whole, or cut each on a sharp angle and fan out the slices. I particularly like to lean the mushrooms against mounds of Carrot, Bean, and Caramelized Shallot Purée (page 87) for a satisfying vegan version of steak and potatoes.

PORTOBELLO "STEAKS"

SERVES 4

2 TABLESPOONS OLIVE OIL, PLUS OIL FOR PREPARING THE PAN

4 LARGE PORTOBELLO MUSHROOM CAPS (5 TO 6 INCHES IN DIAMETER)

1 TABLESPOON JAPANESE SOY SAUCE (SHOYU OR TAMARI)

2 TEASPOONS BALSAMIC VINEGAR

SALT AND FRESHLY GROUND PEPPER

01 Place the rack in the center of the oven and preheat to 450°F. Oil one or two shallow roasting pans large enough to hold the caps in one layer.

02 Lightly wipe the portobello caps with a damp kitchen towel. Remove any stems that prevent the caps from sitting flat in the pan. With the gill sides down, tap the mushrooms gently on the kitchen counter to dislodge any dirt caught in the crevices. Arrange on the roasting pan with gill sides down.

03 In a small bowl, use a fork to combine and emulsify the oil, soy sauce, and vinegar. Liberally brush the mixture onto the tops and sides of the caps. Season with salt and pepper.

04 Roast until the color of the tops and edges deepens, 5 to 6 minutes. Flip over. Give the oil mixture a good stir, and then brush the bottoms. Roast until cooked through and tender (they will look slightly collapsed and yield to the touch), 3 to 5 minutes more. Serve immediately, whole or sliced.

OTHER IDEAS

Sprinkle the portobellos with fresh or dried thyme when seasoning with salt and pepper.

Make roasted portobello sandwiches on split focaccia smeared with Creamy Herb Dressing (page 95) or Parsley Aioli (page 45).

Using collards as wrappers for a savory grain filling provides a welcome opportunity to appreciate their forest green color and artistic veining. When set on a pool of Roasted Red Pepper Sauce, the verdant rolls are fresh and inviting. If your prior encounters with collards have been limited to olive drab puddles drowning in the stewpot, this recipe will introduce you to a new and elegant aspect of this fine vegetable.

Collard bunches inevitably come with leaves of varying sizes. Rather than fight nature, just stuff and roll whatever comes your way until you run out of either leaves or filling. To divide the labor-intensive aspect of this dish, have cooked grains on hand (page 20), and make the Roasted Red Pepper Sauce in advance.

STUFFED **COLLARD** ROLLS WITH ROASTED **RED PEPPER** SAUCE

01 Prepare the Roasted Red Pepper Sauce, and set aside.

02 Cut off the collard stems, and trim any leaves that measure longer than 10 inches from top to stem end. Thinly slice 1 cup of the stems and set aside. (Save the remaining stems for another use.)

03 Select a pot wide and deep enough to contain the collard leaves without bending them too much. Fill it about halfway with water. Add $1/2$ teaspoon of the salt. Bring to a boil.

04 Press the collard leaves into the boiling water. (If necessary, cook in two batches.) Cover and boil until just tender, 5 to 10 minutes. (To test for doneness, use scissors to snip off a small piece of leaf near the stem end; err on the side of undercooking, as the leaves tear more easily if overcooked.)

05 Drain the collard leaves in a colander set over a bowl, reserving the cooking broth. Set the collards under cold running water, gently turning them once or twice, until they are thoroughly cooled. Set aside to drain.

06 Heat the oil in the same pot. Add the leeks and cook over medium-high heat, stirring often, until they wilt, about 3 minutes. Meanwhile crush the fennel seeds using a mortar and pestle, or coarsely chop them with a chef's knife. Add the fennel seeds, celery, carrot,

CONTINUED

SERVES **5 OR 6**

ROASTED RED PEPPER SAUCE (RECIPE FOLLOWS)

1 1/2 TO 2 POUNDS COLLARD GREENS (HAVE AT LEAST 25 LEAVES)

1 TEASPOON SALT, PLUS MORE IF NEEDED

1 TABLESPOON VEGETABLE OIL

2 CUPS FINELY CHOPPED LEEKS

2 TEASPOONS FENNEL SEEDS

3/4 CUP FINELY DICED CELERY

3/4 CUP FINELY DICED CARROT

FRESHLY GROUND BLACK PEPPER

3 CUPS COOKED PEARL BARLEY

2 CUPS COOKED SHORT-GRAIN BROWN RICE OR ADDITIONAL BARLEY

2/3 CUP HAZELNUTS, TOASTED AND COARSELY CHOPPED

1/2 TABLESPOON HAZELNUT OIL, PLUS MORE IF NEEDED

1/3 CUP LOOSELY PACKED CHOPPED FRESH DILL

2 TO 3 TABLESPOONS FRESHLY SQUEEZED LEMON JUICE

reserved collard stems, $1/2$ cup reserved collard broth, the remaining $1/2$ teaspoon salt, and pepper to taste. Cover and cook over medium-high heat until the vegetables are tender but still firm, 8 to 10 minutes. Add more collard broth if the mixture becomes dry.

07 Using a blender or food processor, blend $1/2$ cup of collard broth with 1 cup of barley to create a coarse purée. Add the purée, remaining grains, hazelnuts, hazelnut oil, and dill to the leek mixture. Season to taste with salt and pepper and additional hazelnut oil, if needed. Stir in enough lemon juice to give a distinct lemony edge.

08 To assemble the rolls: Set a collard leaf on a flat surface with the smoother side up and the mid-rib running from left to right (i.e., horizontally). Patch any tears with pieces of another leaf.

09 Mound $1/4$ to $3/4$ cup of the stuffing (depending upon the size of the leaf) just below and along the full length of the mid-rib. Flip the leaf edge closest to you over the filling and roll the leaf up so that the mid-rib runs along its length. (You may also fold in the sides of the leaf to create a packet, as shown on page 66.) Set the roll seam-side down on a microwavable or ovenproof platter. Continue to assemble rolls until you have used up all of the filling or leaves.

10 Just before serving, reheat the rolls in a microwave or in the oven, loosely covered with foil. To serve, ladle Roasted Red Pepper Sauce onto dinner plates, and arrange the rolls on top.

OTHER IDEAS

COLLARD "SPAGHETTI"

Stack any extra cooked collard greens in a pile and roll them tightly into a cigar. Slice thin. Brown slivered garlic in olive oil, add the sliced collards, and cook, tossing frequently, until heated.

Use leftover collard broth as a base for soup. It also makes a soothing hot drink, perhaps seasoned with a drop of soy sauce.

ROASTED **RED PEPPER** SAUCE

01 In a blender or food processor, purée the peppers with the oil, ³/₄ cup of the beans, and the salt.

02 Transfer the purée to a saucepan and stir in the remaining beans. Add more salt if needed and enough Balsamic Syrup to enhance the taste.

03 If the sauce is thin or lacks a finished flavor, bring it to a boil and simmer, stirring frequently, until it has a good consistency and the flavors are integrated. Set aside until needed; reheat when ready to serve.

MAKES ABOUT **3 ¹/₂ CUPS**

3 LARGE RED BELL PEPPERS (ABOUT 1 ³/₄ POUNDS), ROASTED (PAGE 13) AND CUT INTO CHUNKS

2 TABLESPOONS OLIVE OIL

1 ³/₄ CUPS COOKED NAVY BEANS OR ONE 15-OUNCE CAN, DRAINED

¹/₂ TEASPOON SALT, PLUS MORE IF NEEDED

¹/₂ TO 1 TEASPOON BALSAMIC SYRUP (PAGE 16) OR BALSAMIC VINEGAR

THE BASICS

3 CUPS COOKED GRAINS (AT ROOM TEMPERATURE)

1 CUP COOKED BEANS

FOR CRUNCH

1 CUP DICED CARROT, CELERY, BELL PEPPER, SEEDED CUCUMBER, OR FENNEL

1/4 TO 1/2 CUP TOASTED NUTS (CHOPPING OPTIONAL)

1/4 CUP TOASTED SUNFLOWER OR PUMPKIN SEEDS

1 TO 2 TABLESPOONS FLAX SEEDS OR TOASTED SESAME SEEDS

FOR AN HERBAL ACCENT

1/4 TO 1/2 CUP FINELY CHOPPED FRESH PARSLEY, DILL, BASIL, CILANTRO, OR MINT

FOR A POP OF INTENSE FLAVOR

2 TABLESPOONS DRAINED CAPERS

1/4 CUP CHOPPED PITTED OLIVES, PICKLES, OR SUN-DRIED TOMA-TOES (OIL-PACKED)

1/2 CUP THINLY SLICED SCALLION GREENS OR DICED RED ONION

1/2 CUP CHOPPED MARINATED ARTICHOKE HEARTS

1 TO 2 TABLESPOONS CHOPPED, SEEDED JALAPEÑOS

I always turn to this mix-and-match recipe when I need to create an attractive and hearty grain and bean salad from ingredients on hand. If you store cooked grains in the freezer (see page 22) and have a can of beans in the pantry, this salad makes a dandy impromptu lunch or dinner, perhaps accompanied by a green salad.

I usually start my creative plan with whatever fresh herb is available. If it's basil or parsley, for example, I'll make a Mediterranean-inspired salad using brown rice or wheat berries, chickpeas, celery, roasted red pepper, capers, and scallions with a dressing based on olive oil and lemon juice. If I'm starting with cilantro, I'll go the Southwest or Latin route, using quinoa, black beans, toasted pumpkin seeds, pimento-stuffed olives, corn, and red onion, with lime juice in the dressing. Or I'll make an Asian salad with black soybeans, brown rice, red bell pepper, snow peas, scallion greens, toasted sesame seeds, and a dressing of toasted sesame oil, lemon juice, and soy sauce.

Quantities suggested below are approximate and intended as rough guidelines. The idea is to have fun and taste as you go until you arrive at a combination that pleases you. For a pretty salad with varied tastes and textures, plan to toss the grains and beans with at least one ingredient from the categories labeled Crunch, Herbal Accent, and Pop of Intense Flavor. (Leftovers will need perking up with extra acid.)

AS-YOU-PLEASE GRAIN AND BEAN SALAD

01 Toss the grains, beans, and your choice of additional salad ingredients together in a large bowl or storage container.

02 Thoroughly blend your choice of oil, acid, and seasonings in a small jar or bowl.

03 Toss the dressing into the salad. Add more acid or salt, if needed, to create a good balance of flavors. (I like my salads to have an assertive acid component.) Serve at room temperature.

OTHER IDEAS

The oil drained from marinated sun-dried tomatoes is very tasty.

Serve the salad on a bed of greens or shredded cabbage. Red cabbage is especially striking.

Accompany with slices of avocado or tomato seasoned with salt.

If you've used dense whole grains such as wheat berries or kamut, toss in some shredded Romaine to lighten the mixture.

FOR COLOR CONTRAST AND VARIETY (OPTIONAL)

2 TO 4 TABLESPOONS RAISINS, DRIED CURRANTS, OR DRIED CRANBERRIES

½ CUP DICED ROASTED RED PEPPER

1 CUP COOKED CORN OR GREEN PEAS

1 CUP BLANCHED SNOW PEAS, CUT ON THE DIAGONAL

1 CUP CHERRY TOMATOES, HALVED OR QUARTERED

SIMPLE VINAIGRETTE DRESSING

OIL:

2 TABLESPOONS OLIVE OIL, OR 1 TABLESPOON NUT OIL PLUS 1 TABLESPOON NEUTRAL OIL SUCH AS CORN OR PEANUT, OR 1 TABLESPOON TOASTED SESAME OIL

ACID:

2 TO 4 TABLESPOONS FRESHLY SQUEEZED LEMON OR LIME JUICE, OR 1 TO 2 TABLESPOONS WINE VINEGAR

SEASONINGS TO TASTE:

SALT OR JAPANESE SOY SAUCE (SHOYU OR TAMARI)

FRESHLY GROUND PEPPER

DIJON MUSTARD

The spices of the Moroccan kitchen tantalize me time and again. After years of experimenting, I've discovered that they happily marry the ingredients of far-off shores.

A case in point is this brightly colored vegetable stew featuring the sweet, dense, orange-fleshed Japanese pumpkin known as kabocha. Kabocha is a roundish, striped, green-orange squash whose appearance closely resembles a buttercup squash (which can be used as a substitute). Kabochas are almost always available in health-food stores that carry organic produce. Look for one that feels firm and heavy for its size, and chances are you'll be in for a real treat. Kabocha's rind becomes as tender as its flesh, making peeling unnecessary. What more could you ask of a squash?

This stew makes fine company fare. The fragrance of far-away places will welcome guests to your home, and the bright splashes of squash orange and spinach green will bring good cheer. The dish is substantial enough to serve on its own, but couscous makes a natural companion. It's fun to press individual portions of couscous into ramekins or flat-bottomed coffee cups and unmold them on one end of the plate.

KABOCHA **SQUASH** AND **SPINACH** WITH MOROCCAN SPICES

01 Crumble the saffron into a small bowl and pour the water on top. Set aside.

02 Place the coriander and cumin seeds in a small, heavy skillet and set over high heat. Toast, stirring frequently, until the spices emit a fragrance, pop, or begin to darken, 1 to 2 minutes. (Take care not to burn them.) Immediately transfer the seeds to a coffee grinder reserved for this purpose (or use a mortar and pestle). Cool for a minute or two, then grind into a fairly fine powder. Blend in the cinnamon and cayenne. Set aside.

03 In a heavy 5-quart pot, heat the oil. Stir in the red and yellow onion rings and cook over medium-high heat, stirring frequently, until they begin to brown, 4 to 5 minutes. Stir in the ginger and reserved ground spices and cook for 20 seconds. Add the chickpea cooking-liquid, reserved saffron and its soaking water, salt, and a few twists of pepper. Bring to a boil.

04 Stir in the apricots, chickpeas, and squash. Cover and cook over medium heat, stirring occasionally, until the squash is tender but

CONTINUED

SERVES **4**

1/2 **TEASPOON SAFFRON THREADS**

1 **TABLESPOON WATER**

1 1/2 **TABLESPOONS CORIANDER SEEDS**

1 1/2 **TEASPOONS CUMIN SEEDS**

1/4 **TEASPOON GROUND CINNAMON**

PINCH OF CAYENNE (DEPENDING UPON DESIRED HEAT)

2 **TABLESPOONS OLIVE OIL**

1 **LARGE RED ONION (ABOUT 8 OUNCES), THINLY SLICED INTO RINGS**

1 **LARGE YELLOW ONION (ABOUT 8 OUNCES), THINLY SLICED INTO RINGS**

1 1/2 **TABLESPOONS PEELED, MINCED FRESH GINGER**

2 1/2 **CUPS CHICKPEA COOKING-LIQUID (IF IT TASTES GOOD), VEGETABLE BROTH, OR WATER, PLUS MORE IF NEEDED**

1 **TEASPOON SALT**

FRESHLY GROUND PEPPER

10 **DRIED APRICOTS (CUT SOME IN QUARTERS AND OTHERS IN HALF)**

1 1/2 **CUPS COOKED CHICKPEAS OR ONE 15-OUNCE CAN, DRAINED**

2 **POUNDS KABOCHA SQUASH, TRIMMED, SEEDED, AND CUT INTO 1-INCH CHUNKS (OR SUBSTITUTE PEELED BUTTERNUT, BUTTERCUP, OR OTHER WINTER SQUASH)**

10 OUNCES SPINACH, TRIMMED OF THICK STEMS AND TORN INTO BITS

1 TEASPOON GRATED LEMON ZEST

1 TO 2 TABLESPOONS FRESHLY SQUEEZED LEMON JUICE

1/3 CUP SLIVERED TOASTED ALMONDS, FOR GARNISH (OPTIONAL)

still firm, 20 to 35 minutes. (Peeled butternut or buttercup will probably take less time than unpeeled kabocha.) Stir in a bit of broth or water during this time if the mixture becomes dry.

05 Stir in the spinach and lemon zest. Cover and cook just until the spinach is tender, a minute or two. Adjust the seasonings. Just before serving, stir in enough lemon juice to balance the sweetness.

06 The stew will thicken as it stands, but if you wish to thicken the sauce immediately, mash a few pieces of squash against the sides of the pot with a fork, and stir well to blend. Garnish individual portions with slivered almonds, if you wish.

OTHER IDEAS

Substitute pitted prunes for the apricots.

Omit the spinach and cook the squash with 1 pound of Swiss chard, stems thinly sliced and leaves coarsely chopped. Ruby chard is especially pretty.

These flaky phyllo packets get rave reviews, the requisite payoff for a labor-intensive dish. For the unusual filling, cooked kale is combined with allspice-scented leeks, toasted pine nuts, and chewy grains. I also include brewer's yeast (page 14), which lends a savory note to both the filling and the phyllo crust. With a colorful tossed salad, the triangles make a substantial entrée.

Shaping phyllo triangles is much like folding the flag. If using frozen phyllo (available in 1-pound packages at most supermarkets), defrost it according to package directions. You probably won't need the full pound, but it's good to have extra on hand in case of tears. Just lay torn pieces beside each other, as if you were working a jigsaw puzzle. The triangles will still look and taste fine.

Any leftover phyllo can be sandwiched in plastic wrap, loosely rolled up, and then put in a zipper-topped plastic bag. Refrigerate or refreeze. Or consider making the Rustic Apple Tart (page 104), which requires only four sheets of phyllo.

PHYLLO TRIANGLES FILLED WITH **KALE, PINE NUTS,** AND **CURRANTS**

MAKES **8 TRIANGLES**

1/4 CUP DRIED CURRANTS

2 TABLESPOONS BOILING WATER

1 TABLESPOON DRY SHERRY

1 TEASPOON SALT, PLUS MORE TO TASTE

1 POUND KALE

7 TABLESPOONS OLIVE OIL, DIVIDED

1 CUP CHOPPED LEEKS OR ONION

1/2 TEASPOON GROUND ALLSPICE

1 1/2 CUPS COOKED CHEWY GRAINS, SUCH AS WHEAT BERRIES OR SHORT-GRAIN BROWN RICE

1/3 CUP (ABOUT 2 OUNCES) PINE NUTS, TOASTED

2 TABLESPOONS FRESHLY SQUEEZED LEMON JUICE

6 TABLESPOONS LEWIS LABORATORIES BREWER'S YEAST, DIVIDED

FRESHLY GROUND PEPPER

1 POUND PHYLLO (ALSO SPELLED FILO)

01 Place the currants in a small bowl and add the boiling water and sherry. Cover and set aside.

02 Fill a 6-quart pot about three-fourths full of water and add the salt. Bring to a boil. Holding the kale in a bunch, trim off and discard about an inch at the bottom of the stems. Thinly slice the remaining stems and leaves.

03 Add the kale to the boiling water in several batches, submerging each batch under the water with a large, long-handled spoon. Cover and cook over high heat until the kale is tender, 5 to 8 minutes. Pour the kale into a colander to drain, reserving the cooking liquid if you wish. Set the kale under cold running water to stop the cooking process. Set aside to continue draining.

04 In a nonstick skillet, heat 1 tablespoon of the oil. Stir in the leeks, allspice, and a generous pinch of salt. Cover and cook over medium-low heat until the leeks are tender, about 10 minutes. Add the currants and any unabsorbed soaking liquid and cook uncovered over high heat, stirring constantly, until all of the liquid has evaporated, another minute or two. Set aside.

CONTINUED

05 Squeeze small amounts of the cooked kale between your palms to extract as much liquid as possible. Place the squeezed kale in the bowl of a food processor as you go. Process the kale until finely chopped. Transfer the kale to a bowl and stir in the reserved leeks, grains, pine nuts, lemon juice, and 2 tablespoons of the brewer's yeast. Season well with salt and pepper. (You can refrigerate the filling until needed, but bring it back to room temperature before assembling the packets.)

06 Place 2 racks in the lower half of the oven, and preheat the oven to 425°F. Line 2 baking sheets with parchment paper and set aside. Wet a lightweight kitchen towel and thoroughly wring out the excess water. Place the remaining 6 tablespoons of olive oil and remaining brewer's yeast in separate small bowls, and have them nearby.

07 To assemble the triangles: Unwrap the phyllo and unroll it onto a clean flat surface. Immediately cover the pile of phyllo completely with the damp kitchen towel to prevent it from drying out and becoming brittle.

08 Gently peel off 1 sheet of phyllo and set it on a flat surface. Replace the damp towel over the remaining phyllo. Working rapidly, use a pastry brush to lightly coat the phyllo with olive oil. Sprinkle with a scant teaspoon of brewer's yeast. Lay a second sheet on top and brush with more oil and sprinkle with yeast. Fold the 2 sheets in half lengthwise to create a rectangle.

09 Have the longer side of the rectangle running horizontally. Set ½ cup of filling about an inch from the left edge. Fold the bottom left corner of the phyllo up over the filling to encase the filling in a triangular shape. Press the edges of the triangle to seal the filling inside. Brush the top surface with oil and sprinkle with brewer's yeast.

10 Gently lift the triangle and fold it over to the right to maintain the triangular shape. Continue folding, brushing, and sprinkling until you reach the end, usually 4 folds in all. Trim off any excess phyllo and brush the top with oil. Continue with the remaining phyllo and filling, placing triangles in a single layer on the parchment paper as you go.

11 Bake until the edges are crisp and golden brown, 8 to 10 minutes. If you'd like the tops browner, set the triangles about 4 inches from the broiling element for a minute or two. Watch very carefully, as the phyllo burns easily. Serve hot.

OLIVE OIL FOR PREPARING PANS AND DRIZZLING OVER FENNEL

2 POUNDS PLUM TOMATOES, QUARTERED LENGTHWISE

SALT

2 MEDIUM FENNEL BULBS OR 1 LARGE BULB (ABOUT 1 ½ POUNDS WEIGHED WITH STALKS)

1 TO 2 TABLESPOONS EXTRA-VIRGIN OLIVE OIL

1 TO 2 TEASPOONS BALSAMIC SYRUP (PAGE 16), FOR GARNISH (OPTIONAL)

To prepare this simple side-dish salad, you roast plum tomatoes and fennel in a 250°F oven, and then arrange them attractively on small plates. Season them simply, with just a drizzle of salt and your best extra-virgin olive oil.

The dish requires only a few minutes of preparation but two to three hours of cooking. I developed it specifically to be made with and served alongside the Slow-Baked Cannellini with Olives, Escarole, and Gremolata (page 63).

Two pounds of plum tomatoes yields about 2 cups roasted, enough to serve 4 to 6 as part of this side dish. Why not double the amount to have some on hand for garnishes (great on sandwiches) or to serve with the Hiziki Tapenade (page 28)? Refrigerated in a well-sealed container, they last about 10 days.

SLOW-ROASTED **TOMATOES** AND **FENNEL**

01 Preheat the oven to 250°F. Select one or two baking sheets large enough to arrange the tomatoes in one layer and brush with oil. Arrange the tomatoes on the sheets cut side up and sprinkle them lightly with salt. Set aside.

02 Select a heavy roasting pan or large gratin dish for the fennel (it does not have to fit in a single layer), and brush the bottom with oil. Remove any fennel fronds and set aside for garnish. Cut the top stalks from the fennel and reserve for stock. Trim the base, and quarter each bulb, top to base. Discard any tough or bruised outer layers. Slice the quartered bulbs ¼ inch thick, leaving the core as intact as possible to hold the layers together. (This won't be possible with all of the slices.) Set in the roasting pan, seasoning lightly with salt and drizzling with olive oil as you go. Cover the pan tightly with foil.

03 Bake the tomatoes until collapsed and shriveled, 2 to 2 ½ hours. (For the first hour or so, it will look like nothing is happening.) At the same time, bake the fennel until tender and easily pierced with the tip of a paring knife, 1 ½ to 2 hours. (Once the fennel is tender, you can roast it uncovered to brown it and achieve a more intense flavor.)

04 To serve, arrange the fennel and tomatoes decoratively on small plates and drizzle with extra-virgin olive oil. Finely chop the reserved fennel fronds and use them as a garnish. If you wish, dot a few drops of Balsamic Syrup decoratively around the plate.

The next time you spot a large cauliflower and a healthy bunch of fresh basil, try this festive dish. Steam the cauliflower whole and drape it decoratively with basil pesto and a crown of sun-dried tomato pesto. Cut the wedges as you would a cake so everyone gets a taste of both sauces.

The pestos will adhere to the cauliflower only if it has cooled down completely, so plan to serve this dish at room temperature. It's important to spin-dry the basil leaves thoroughly to avoid having a pesto that is too watery to give the cauliflower a nice, thick coating.

RED, WHITE, AND GREEN **CAULIFLOWER**

1 LARGE HEAD CAULIFLOWER (2 1/2 TO 3 POUNDS BEFORE TRIMMING)

2 LARGE CLOVES ROASTED GARLIC OR 1 SMALL CLOVE RAW GARLIC

1 CUP WALNUTS, LIGHTLY TOASTED

2 TABLESPOONS OLIVE OIL

2 TABLESPOONS FRESHLY SQUEEZED LEMON JUICE

1 TEASPOON SALT

1 TABLESPOON LEWIS LABORATORIES BREWER'S YEAST (PAGE 14; OPTIONAL BUT HIGHLY RECOMMENDED)

2 CUPS VERY TIGHTLY PACKED BASIL LEAVES, RINSED AND SPUN DRY

1/4 CUP SUN-DRIED TOMATOES (OIL-PACKED)

01 Slice off the base and large leaves of the cauliflower. Use a paring knife to cut away the smaller leaves and expose the base of the florets. Even off the bottom so that the cauliflower will sit upright.

02 Pour an inch of water into a pot tall enough to hold the cauliflower upright. Bring the water to a boil. Set the cauliflower in the water, cover, and steam over high heat until you can easily slip a paring knife 2 inches deep into the florets, 8 to 10 minutes. (The cauliflower should be tender but still firm.)

03 Transfer the cauliflower to a colander and run cold water over it to hasten cooling. Set aside to cool further, or refrigerate overnight.

04 To make the pestos, pop the garlic through the feed tube of a food processor with the motor running. Add the walnuts, oil, lemon juice, salt, and brewer's yeast (if using). Process to create a coarse paste.

05 Transfer 3 tablespoons of this paste to a small bowl and set aside. Add the basil leaves to the processor bowl and process to make the basil pesto, adjusting seasonings and scraping the bowl as needed. Transfer to a small bowl. Scrape down the processor bowl thoroughly or wipe it clean. Blend the sun-dried tomatoes with the remaining 3 tablespoons of walnut paste.

06 Set the cauliflower on a serving platter. Blot it completely dry with a towel. Using a rubber spatula and your fingers (this will remind you of finger painting), spread a circle of sun-dried tomato pesto on the top of the cauliflower. Coat the remainder of the cauliflower with the basil pesto. To serve, halve the cauliflower, then cut into thick wedges.

SERVES 4

1 TO 2 TABLESPOONS VEGETABLE OIL
(OLIVE, HERB-INFUSED, ROASTED
PEANUT, TOASTED SESAME, CORN)

2 CUPS COARSELY CHOPPED YELLOW
OR RED ONIONS, LEEKS, SHAL-
LOTS, OR SCALLION BULBS

1/2 TO 1 CUP DICED CELERY
(OPTIONAL)

1 TO 2 CLOVES GARLIC, MINCED
(OPTIONAL)

1/4 TO 1 TEASPOON DRIED HERBS

1/2 TO 1 1/2 CUPS WATER OR VEG-
ETABLE BROTH

3 CUPS COOKED GRAINS (ONE TYPE
OR A MEDLEY; SEE PAGE 22)

SALT AND FRESHLY GROUND PEPPER

OPTIONAL ADD-ONS

FROZEN PEAS OR CORN

CHOPPED, COOKED VEGETABLES OR
COOKED BEANS

SAUTÉED SLICED MUSHROOMS

DRIED CURRANTS, RAISINS, OR
CRANBERRIES

1/4 TO 1/2 CUP CHOPPED FRESH HERBS

A FEW TABLESPOONS TOASTED NUTS

A DRIZZLE OF BALSAMIC SYRUP
(PAGE 16) TO ENHANCE FLAVOR

SNIPPED FRESH CHIVES OR SCALLION
GREENS, FOR GARNISH
(OPTIONAL)

Use this recipe as a template for sprucing up leftover or frozen cooked grains (page 22). The main flavor provider is browned onions (or another member of the allium family), chopped coarsely so that they have a distinct presence in the finished dish.

Depending upon the seasonings and the number of add-ons you choose, you'll end up with either a side-dish grain that complements the rest of your meal or a medley substantial enough to serve as the entrée.

For example, if I were serving the grains to accompany an Italian meal, I'd use olive oil, scent the mixture with dried oregano, and add toasted, chopped hazelnuts. For a quick Southwestern supper, I'd sauté red onion with ground cumin and then add black beans, corn, toasted pumpkin seeds, and chopped fresh cilantro. For Asian grains, I'd cook the onions in 1 tablespoon of toasted sesame oil and use soy sauce instead of salt, adding cooked edamame (green soy beans) at the end.

If you are starting with frozen cooked grains, place them in a colander or strainer and pour boiling water over them to break up the blocks and partially defrost them before you proceed. For a pleasing presentation, press the savory grains into a ramekin and unmold one or two onto each plate.

SAVORY GRAINS

01 In a large, nonstick skillet, heat the oil. Add the onions, celery, and garlic (if using), and cook over medium heat, stirring frequently, until the onions are wilted and beginning to brown, 4 to 6 minutes. Crumble in the minimum amount of dried herbs and continue cooking until the onions are nicely browned, about 5 minutes more.

02 Stir in 1/2 cup of water and the grains. Season with salt, pepper, and additional herbs to taste. When the mixture starts to sizzle, turn down the heat, cover, and cook over low heat until the grains are moist and heated throughout, 2 to 3 minutes. Stir in more water during this time if the grains taste dry or begin sticking to the skillet.

03 At the last minute, stir in any frozen or cooked vegetables and beans, and continue cooking until heated throughout. Just before serving, stir in dried fruit, fresh herbs, or nuts (if using). Season with Balsamic Syrup and garnish with chives, if you wish.

Pommes Anna minus all the butter, cream, and fat? This potato cake is a tasty vegan alternative, made by baking thinly sliced Yukon Golds that have been pressed down firmly into a cake tin by the weight of a heavy, water-filled pot. The potatoes are seasoned with a savory, "cheesy" blend of brewer's yeast (page 14), salt, and pepper.

The cake is easy to assemble. Leave the potato peels intact for added flavor, and use the 1/8-inch slicing disk of the food processor to make quick work of the preparation. (Or slice the potatoes as thinly as you can by hand.) If you use a springform pan, you'll be able to unmold the potato cake before slicing it into wedges; otherwise, just serve the wedges from the pan.

POTATO CAKE

01 Place a rack in the lower third of the oven and preheat to 450°F. Liberally coat the bottom and sides of an 8- or 9-inch cake pan or springform pan with some of the oil. To weigh down the potato cake, locate a heavy pot or ovenproof casserole that will fit into the pan.

02 In a small bowl, combine the brewer's yeast, salt, and pepper. Set aside.

03 Using the thinnest slicing disk of your food processor, slice the potatoes. Arrange a fairly even layer of slices in the bottom of the pan. Sprinkle some of the brewer's yeast mixture on top. Repeat this process, creating a total of 6 or 7 layers and ending with a sprinkling of the brewer's yeast mixture on top. Drizzle on the remaining olive oil.

04 Lay 2 large sheets of aluminum foil on top of the pan. Set the heavy pot on top and firmly press it into the potatoes. Seal the cake pan well by pressing the overhanging foil tightly to the sides and under the bottom. If using a springform pan, set it on a foil-lined baking sheet to catch any drips.

05 Transfer to the oven and fill the pot halfway with water to make it heavier still. Bake until the center of the "cake" offers no resistance when pierced (right through the foil) with a paring knife, about 1 hour.

CONTINUED

SERVES **4 TO 6**

OLIVE OIL FOR PREPARING THE PAN, PLUS 1 TABLESPOON ADDITIONAL

1/4 CUP LEWIS LABORATORIES BREWER'S YEAST

1 1/4 TEASPOONS SALT

1/4 TEASPOON FRESHLY GROUND BLACK PEPPER

2 POUNDS YUKON GOLD POTATOES, TRIMMED OF BLEMISHES (DRY OFF AFTER RINSING)

06 Preheat the broiler. Remove the foil and set the "cake" about 5 inches beneath the broiler until the top is lightly browned and crisp, 2 to 5 minutes. Let cool for 5 minutes.

07 If you've used a springform pan, run a knife along the edges and remove the ring. Leave the "cake" on the base and transfer to a platter. If you've used a cake pan, cut the "cake" into wedges and serve directly from the pan. Serve hot.

OTHER IDEAS

Increase the ground pepper to a scant $\frac{1}{2}$ teaspoon for a distinctively peppery accent. Use a fine-quality black pepper, such as Malabar or Telicherry.

Rub the bottom and sides of the oiled baking pan with the cut side of a clove of garlic. Scatter a few whole peeled garlic cloves on top of the assembled "cake." (Minced and granulated garlic don't work well in this recipe.)

Cut 8 to 10 thin slices of red onion and break them into rings. Scatter the rings on top of the raw potato cake and drizzle with olive oil. Proceed to cover and bake as directed. Take care when browning under the broiler, as the onions burn easily.

Carrots give this comfort-food purée an attractive, pale, autumn orange color. Caramelized shallots add earthy depth and balance the carrots' sweetness, while white beans contribute their buttery smooth texture. If you have the impression that shallots are no more than "onions with an attitude," this recipe may change your mind. I like to serve this purée with Portobello "Steaks" (page 65).

CARROT, BEAN, AND CARAMELIZED SHALLOT PURÉE

SERVES **3 OR 4**

3 TABLESPOONS OLIVE OIL

1 1/2 CUPS CHOPPED SHALLOTS (8 OUNCES)

1/2 TEASPOON DRIED SAVORY LEAVES, PLUS MORE IF NEEDED

12 OUNCES CARROTS, PEELED AND CUT INTO 3/4-INCH CHUNKS

1 3/4 CUPS COOKED WHITE BEANS, SUCH AS CANNELLINI OR NAVY, OR ONE 15-OUNCE CAN, DRAINED

1 CUP VEGETABLE BROTH

1/2 TEASPOON SALT

FRESHLY GROUND PEPPER TO TASTE

01 Heat the oil in a large, heavy skillet. Add the shallots and savory and cook over medium-low heat at a gentle sizzle, stirring occasionally, until the shallots turn golden brown, 20 to 25 minutes.

02 While the shallots are cooking, steam the carrots until very tender, 10 to 12 minutes. Leave the carrots in the covered pot and set aside off the heat.

03 When the shallots are golden brown, add the beans, broth, salt, and pepper. Bring to a boil. Add more savory, if you wish. Cover and simmer over medium heat until the beans taste lightly seasoned, about 10 minutes. If the mixture is soupy, boil it over high heat, stirring frequently, until most of the liquid evaporates and the mixture becomes thick and porridgelike.

04 Combine the steamed carrots and the bean-shallot mixture in a food processor or blender and purée. Adjust the seasonings. Reheat in the microwave if necessary.

OTHER IDEAS

Thin the purée with homemade vegetable broth and serve as a soup.

Substitute dried tarragon for the savory. Start with 1/8 teaspoon, and add more if needed. Or add chopped fresh tarragon after cooking.

It goes without saying that beets are a gorgeous color. Baking them in individual foil packets develops a flavor intensity to match their brilliant hue and makes it easy to slip off their skins—an ingenious technique discovered by produce specialist Elizabeth Schneider.

Since diced red beets bleed like crazy, they dye the rice a striking hot pink. To avoid getting beet stains under your fingernails, wear rubber gloves when handling them. The light dressing of olive oil and lemon juice calls for just a hint of raspberry vinegar to enhance the beets' natural sweetness.

A few tips: Use your most delicate extra-virgin olive oil, one that will not distract from the beet flavor. (My favorite is the Ligurian Roi available by mail from Zingerman's.) Opt for short-grain brown rice, which has a chewier and more interesting texture than the long-grain variety.

You can turn this side salad into a light lunch entrée by serving it on a bed of Boston (butter) lettuce, with a few slices of avocado on the side.

BAKED **BEET** AND **BROWN RICE** SALAD

1 POUND RED BEETS (3 MEDIUM)

2 ½ CUPS COOKED SHORT-GRAIN BROWN RICE (PAGE 21)

2 TABLESPOONS EXTRA-VIRGIN OLIVE OIL

1 TABLESPOON FRESHLY SQUEEZED LEMON JUICE

1 TEASPOON RASPBERRY VINEGAR, PLUS MORE IF NEEDED

¼ TEASPOON SALT, PLUS MORE IF NEEDED

2 TABLESPOONS THINLY SLICED SCALLION GREENS (OPTIONAL)

2 TABLESPOONS PINE NUTS, FOR GARNISH

01 Preheat the oven to 375°F. Trim off any beet greens, leaving about a half-inch of stem intact. Rinse the beets. Wrap each beet individually in a tightly sealed aluminum foil packet. Set the beets on a foil-lined baking pan and bake until you can easily pierce them to the center with a cake tester or paring knife, 60 to 90 minutes. (You can pierce the beets right through the foil.)

02 When they are cool enough to handle, gently rub the foil of each still-sealed packet against the skin of each beet. Slip off the beet skins along with the foil. Trim off the tail and stems ends. Cut the beets into ¼-inch dice and set them in a bowl or storage container. Add the rice and toss until the rice is "dyed" beet red.

03 In a small bowl, whisk together the oil, lemon juice, vinegar, and salt. Toss the dressing with the beets. Adjust the seasonings, adding more vinegar and/or salt, if needed, to intensify the flavors. Let the salad sit until the grains absorb some flavor, about 15 minutes. Stir in the scallion greens (if using) just before serving. Garnish with pine nuts. Serve at room temperature.

MANGO CHUTNEY DRESSING

3 TABLESPOONS SWEET MANGO CHUTNEY

3 TABLESPOONS FRESHLY SQUEEZED LIME JUICE

2 TABLESPOONS PEANUT BUTTER

2 TO 3 TABLESPOONS WATER

1 TEASPOON SALT

CARROT SLAW

1 POUND CARROTS, PEELED AND SHREDDED (ABOUT 4 CUPS)

1/2 CUP CHOPPED CILANTRO

1/3 CUP THINLY SLICED SCALLION GREENS

ADDITIONAL LIME JUICE, IF NEEDED

ADDITIONAL SALT, IF NEEDED

1/4 CUP CHOPPED ROASTED, SALTED PEANUTS, FOR GARNISH (OPTIONAL)

Mango chutney gives the tart-sweet dressing for this slaw a mysterious complexity. Use your favorite chutney or try Patak's brand, which is widely available and very tasty.

Although I designed this salad to accompany either the Tomato-Chickpea Curry in Eggplant Shells (page 57) or the Skillet Grain Medley with Curried Tempeh (page 48), it is versatile enough to serve at a picnic or a potluck.

CARROT SLAW WITH MANGO CHUTNEY DRESSING

01 In a blender, purée the dressing ingredients, using 2 tablespoons of water, until very smooth. Blend in additional water if the dressing is too thick to coat the carrots.

02 In a large bowl, toss the carrots, cilantro, and scallions with the dressing. Add more lime juice and salt, if needed. Garnish with peanuts, if you wish.

12 OUNCES (1 ½ CUPS) SILKEN-SOFT TOFU

2 LARGE CUCUMBERS (ABOUT 12 OUNCES EACH), PEELED AND CUT INTO CHUNKS

4 TO 5 TABLESPOONS FRESHLY SQUEEZED LIME JUICE

1 TABLESPOON NEUTRAL OIL, SUCH AS CORN OR CANOLA

1 CUP TIGHTLY PACKED FRESH MINT LEAVES

½ CUP TIGHTLY PACKED CILANTRO LEAVES

½ TEASPOON DIJON MUSTARD, PLUS MORE IF NEEDED

1 ¾ TEASPOONS SALT, PLUS MORE IF NEEDED

Inspired by the yogurt-based raitas of India, I created this pale green, frothy sauce with soft tofu rather than the traditional yogurt. When my friends from Bombay gave it their thumbs up, I felt even more convinced about tofu's potential to please those who wish to include more soy in their diets or avoid dairy products.

I created this sauce to serve alongside the Skillet Grain Medley with Curried Tempeh (page 48), where it creates a refreshing counterpart to the dense texture of the grains. Prepare it at least a half hour in advance to give the flavors a chance to meld.

Be sure to use standard, watery cucumbers—not the burpless kind—and don't remove the seeds.

CUCUMBER-MINT "RAITA"

01 In a blender, purée the tofu, cucumbers, 4 tablespoons of the lime juice, oil, mint, cilantro, mustard, and salt. Adjust the seasonings to your taste by adding more mustard, lime juice, and salt.

02 Refrigerate the mixture for at least ½ hour before serving. It keeps well for up to 3 days.

OTHER IDEAS

Serve chilled as a refreshing hot-weather soup. Or thin slightly with water and serve as a drink.

Use as a salad dressing for greens or sliced tomatoes.

This zesty sauce has the texture of mayonnaise and is quite versatile. It makes a tasty topping for Crisp Tortilla Stacks with Roasted Corn and Black Beans (page 43), a good dressing for slaw, and a fine dip for corn chips. In fact, its taste and olive color are reminiscent of guacamole.

The creamy, rich base of the sauce is silken-soft tofu, but that can be the cook's secret, since the cilantro and garlic dominate, with the sun-dried tomatoes contributing an additional layer of flavor. One small clove of garlic creates the right balance for me, but serious garlic lovers will want more.

Although it lasts a few days, the sauce tastes best when freshly made.

SILKEN **CILANTRO** SAUCE

MAKES **1 ³/₄ CUPS**

1 ¹/₂ TABLESPOONS OLIVE OIL OR OIL FROM SUN-DRIED TOMATOES

1 SMALL SHALLOT, CHOPPED

1 OR 2 SMALL CLOVES GARLIC, CHOPPED

1 TO 1 ¹/₄ TEASPOONS SALT

12 OUNCES (1 ¹/₂ CUPS) SILKEN-SOFT TOFU

2 CUPS TIGHTLY PACKED CILANTRO LEAVES AND TENDER STEMS (1 GOOD-SIZED BUNCH)

¹/₄ CUP CHOPPED SUN-DRIED TOMA-TOES (OIL-PACKED)

1 TO 2 TABLESPOONS FRESHLY SQUEEZED LIME JUICE

01 Place the ingredients in a blender in the order listed, using the smaller amounts of salt and lime juice. Purée until very smooth, about 1 minute. Add more salt and lime juice, if needed, to give the sauce a good balance of flavors.

02 Use immediately or refrigerate in a tightly covered container up to 3 days. Stir well before each use. Thin with lime juice or water if the sauce becomes too thick.

¾ CUP (6 OUNCES) SILKEN-SOFT TOFU

2 TABLESPOONS JAPANESE SOY SAUCE (SHOYU OR TAMARI)

2 TABLESPOONS FRESHLY SQUEEZED LEMON JUICE

1 TABLESPOON TOASTED (ASIAN) SESAME OIL

1 CUP TIGHTLY PACKED, CHOPPED WATERCRESS STEMS (LEFT OVER FROM 1 AVERAGE BUNCH)

I usually whip up this dressing when I've made the Split-Pea Soup with Shiitake and Star Anise (page 36) and have watercress stems left over. The spiciness of the watercress is nicely balanced by the toasted sesame oil, and the tofu provides a creamy base. Lemon juice and soy sauce were made for each other—it just took Western cooks a few millennia to realize it.

This dressing is quite versatile and works well with all kinds of salads: green, bean, pasta, and grain. Think of it when you need a salad to accompany Asian-inspired dishes. Double the recipe if you're serving a crowd.

SESAME-WATERCRESS DRESSING

01 In a blender or food processor, purée the ingredients until smooth and creamy, about 1 minute. Adjust seasonings.

02 Refrigerate in a tightly sealed container for up to 3 days. Stir well before each use. Thin with water or additional lemon juice if the mixture becomes too thick.

OTHER IDEAS

Serve as a topping for baked potatoes or steamed vegetables.

After tossing a salad with this dressing, garnish with toasted black or beige sesame seeds.

In this versatile recipe, lemon juice and fresh herbs mask tofu's slight beany taste. Most people will be surprised to learn that tofu is providing creaminess without the cream. Make the dressing with whatever herb matches your meal or mood.

CREAMY **HERB** DRESSING

01 Purée the ingredients in a blender or food processor until very smooth, using 1 tablespoon lemon juice. Add more lemon juice and salt, if needed.

02 Use immediately or refrigerate in a tightly sealed container for up to 3 days. (The vibrant color will become olive drab, but the taste will not be affected.) Stir well before each use. Thin with lemon juice or water if the dressing becomes too thick.

½ *CUP (4 OUNCES) SILKEN-SOFT TOFU*

3 TABLESPOONS OLIVE OIL

2 TABLESPOONS WATER

1 TO 1 ½ *TABLESPOONS FRESHLY SQUEEZED LEMON JUICE*

½ *CUP TIGHTLY PACKED FRESH HERBS, SUCH AS BASIL, DILL, PARSLEY, OR CILANTRO*

½ *TEASPOON SALT, PLUS MORE IF NEEDED*

CHAPTER SEVEN

SWEET **BEGINNINGS** AND **ENDINGS**

1 ⅓ CUPS SOYMILK (NOT THE LIGHT VARIETY), PLUS MORE IF NEEDED

1 ½ TABLESPOONS FRESHLY SQUEEZED LEMON JUICE

1 ¼ CUPS WHOLE WHEAT PASTRY (NOT BREAD!) FLOUR, PLUS MORE IF NEEDED

½ CUP CORNMEAL

¾ TEASPOON SALT

½ TEASPOON BAKING SODA

½ TEASPOON BAKING POWDER

½ TEASPOON GROUND CINNAMON

3 TABLESPOONS NEUTRAL OIL, SUCH AS CORN OR CANOLA, PLUS ADDITIONAL OIL OR PAN SPRAY FOR GREASING THE WAFFLE IRON

2 TABLESPOONS MAPLE SYRUP

Eating homemade waffles for breakfast or brunch always feels like a special treat, and they make a delightful midafternoon snack as well. Vegan waffles are surprisingly light and crisp. Adding cornmeal to the batter gives them extra crunch.

For carefree waffle making, use a nonstick waffle iron, and oil it lightly between batches. Waffles steam and get soggy if stacked on a plate and kept waiting. If you're not eating them right away, either keep them warm in a 200°F oven or cool them completely on a rack and refrigerate or freeze until needed. (Waffles are good keepers.) Defrost and heat the waffles in a toaster or toaster oven.

Serve the waffles with maple syrup and your choice of fresh berries, sliced bananas, or Baked Peaches and Blueberries with Crisp Pecan Topping (page 101).

WHOLEGRAIN WAFFLES

01 In a 2-cup liquid measure, combine the soymilk and lemon juice. Set aside. (The mixture will curdle.)

02 Set a large strainer or sifter over a bowl. Measure in the flour, cornmeal, salt, baking soda, baking powder, and cinnamon. Stir or sift the dry ingredients into the bowl.

03 Stir the oil and maple syrup into the soymilk. Make a well in the center of the dry ingredients and add the liquid. Stir with a fork just until blended. The batter should be medium-thick but still pourable; if it's too runny, stir in a tablespoon or two more flour. Alternatively, if the batter becomes very thick as it stands, stir in a tablespoon or two of soymilk.

04 When the waffle iron is ready, brush the top and bottom with oil or mist with pan spray. Pour a generous ½ cup of batter over the surface. Bake according to manufacturer's directions until crisp, usually 5 to 6 minutes. Serve immediately or transfer to a cooling rack and keep warm in the oven while you are preparing the remaining waffles.

OTHER IDEAS

Add 2 tablespoons of shelled, unsalted sunflower seeds to the batter.

3 CUPS SOYMILK

**3 TABLESPOONS MAPLE SYRUP, PLUS
MORE IF NEEDED**

1/2 TEASPOON VANILLA EXTRACT

1/2 TEASPOON GROUND GINGER

1/2 TEASPOON GROUND CINNAMON

PINCH FRESHLY GRATED NUTMEG

1/8 TEASPOON SALT

**1/2 CUP QUICK-COOKING POLENTA
(THE KIND THAT COOKS IN LESS
THAN 5 MINUTES)**

**1/4 CUP RAISINS, DRIED CRAN-
BERRIES, OR DRIED BLUEBERRIES**

**12 TOASTED WALNUT OR PECAN
HALVES TOSSED IN 1 TABLESPOON
MAPLE SYRUP, FOR GARNISH**

It's 4 o'clock on a cold winter Saturday, and I just had a steaming bowl of sweet polenta. It's the kind of comfort food that quickly warms a person up.

Although polenta reheats fairly well in the microwave, I enjoy it most when freshly made and still piping hot. Others disagree and like it equally well at room temperature. Fortunately, thanks to instant (quick-cooking) polenta, you can whip up a fresh batch in about five minutes. Try it for breakfast as well as dessert.

SWEET **POLENTA** WITH MAPLE-GLAZED **WALNUTS**

01 Pour the soymilk into a heavy saucepan and set over medium-high heat. Whisk in the maple syrup, vanilla, spices, salt, polenta, and raisins.

02 Bring to a boil (but take care, because soymilk easily boils over). Reduce the heat and boil gently. Adjust maple syrup and seasonings to your taste. Whisk frequently until the polenta develops a porridgelike consistency but is still runny and pourable, about 3 minutes. (Avoid overcooking, which will make the polenta stodgy.)

03 Ladle into individual ramekins or dessert bowls. Garnish with maple-glazed walnuts. Serve immediately.

OTHER IDEAS

Omit the nut garnish. While still hot, top each portion with a square or two (or three) of your favorite dark chocolate. As the chocolate melts, swirl it into the polenta.

Substitute your favorite pumpkin pie spice mix for the spices. Stir in chopped crystallized ginger or candied orange peel.

Add a tablespoon of molasses, which will darken the mix and make it reminiscent of Indian pudding.

Serve with Creamy Hazelnut Topping (page 112).

Garnish with toasted (unsalted) sunflower seeds instead of walnuts.

This homey variation of a deep-dish fruit pie offers lovely juxtapositions of tastes, colors, and textures. Pecan halves form a kind of top crust and provide crisp contrast to the soft fruit. This recipe works surprisingly well with frozen fruit, which offers the convenience of peaches that are already peeled and sliced.

Since personal taste and the sweetness of individual fruits vary, I've suggested a range of added sugar. Serve warm or chilled, on its own or with a scoop of nondairy ice cream. Alternatively, use as a topping for waffles or breakfast porridge.

BAKED **PEACHES** AND **BLUEBERRIES** WITH CRISP **PECAN** TOPPING

SERVES **8**

ONE 10- OR 12-OUNCE PACKAGE FROZEN BLUEBERRIES OR 2 CUPS FRESH BERRIES, PICKED OVER AND RINSED

TWO 16- OR 20-OUNCE PACKAGES FROZEN SLICED PEACHES OR 9 CUPS (LOOSELY PACKED) PEELED, PITTED, AND SLICED RIPE FREESTONE PEACHES

1/4 CUP QUICK-COOKING TAPIOCA (GRANULATED OR INSTANT)

1/3 TO 2/3 CUP SUGAR

2 TABLESPOONS FRESHLY SQUEEZED LEMON JUICE

2 TO 3 TEASPOONS GRATED LEMON ZEST

1/2 TEASPOON GROUND CARDAMOM (OPTIONAL)

1 1/2 CUPS PECAN OR WALNUT HALVES

01 Set the rack in the middle of the oven and preheat to 400°F.

02 In a large bowl, toss together the blueberries and peaches (plus any juices they've released), tapioca, sugar, lemon juice, lemon zest, and cardamom (if using). Transfer to a 2-quart (or slightly larger) baking dish. Distribute the pecans on top. Set the pan on a foil-lined baking sheet to catch spills if the fruit bubbles over.

03 Bake until the fruit is tender and the juices are thickened and bubbly, 35 to 45 minutes. If the nuts begin to burn before the fruit is done, cover the top loosely with aluminum foil.

04 Set on a rack and cool for about 10 minutes before serving.

2 ¹/₂ CUPS WATER

¹/₈ TEASPOON SALT

**1 CUP ARBORIO OR VALENCIA SHORT-
GRAIN WHITE RICE**

**2 ¹/₂ CUPS UNFLAVORED SOYMILK
(NOT THE LIGHT VARIETY)**

**¹/₂ TO 1 CUP UNSWEETENED COCOA
POWDER (SCHARFFEN BERGER
AND DROSTE ARE GOOD BRANDS;
ALSO SEE OTHER GOOD THINGS,
PAGE 14.)**

³/₄ TO 1 CUP SUGAR

**3 TABLESPOONS CASHEW OR
ALMOND BUTTER**

**2 TEASPOONS INSTANT COFFEE
POWDER (OPTIONAL, BUT
DEEPENS THE CHOCOLATE
FLAVOR)**

**CREAMY HAZELNUT TOPPING
(PAGE 112; OPTIONAL)**

**TOASTED SLIVERED ALMONDS OR
VEGAN CHOCOLATE CHIPS, FOR
GARNISH (OPTIONAL)**

For chocoholics who are also fans of rice pudding, this dessert offers the best of both worlds.

To achieve the creamiest possible texture, use full-fat soymilk and a starchy, short-grain, chubby white rice like Valencia paella rice (relatively inexpensive and available in many supermarkets under the Goya label) or Arborio risotto rice.

Since cocoa powder is virtually fat-free, the pudding tastes slightly grainy unless you include some luscious nut butter in the mix (though you won't actually taste it). I've given ranges of amounts for the cocoa powder and sugar to accommodate different brands and preferences.

The pudding provides diverse experiences of pleasure when served hot, at room temperature, or chilled. Creamy Hazelnut Topping (page 112) complements it nicely.

CHOCOLATE RICE PUDDING

01 In a heavy 3-quart saucepan, bring the water and salt to a boil. Add the rice. Cover and cook over low heat until the rice is quite soft and most or all of the water has been absorbed, 25 to 30 minutes.

02 While the rice is cooking, in a blender combine the soymilk with the minimum amounts of cocoa powder and sugar, the cashew butter, and the instant coffee powder (if using). Process until all of the nut butter is completely blended in, about 1 minute. Taste and add more cocoa and/or sugar, if you wish. (Keep in mind that the flavor and sweetness will be somewhat diminished after the liquid is cooked with the rice.)

03 Stir the chocolate mixture into the cooked rice. Bring to a boil over high heat. (Take care, as soymilk easily boils over.) Then lower the heat and cook uncovered at a gentle boil, stirring frequently to prevent the rice from sticking to the bottom of the pot and to break up any skin that forms on top. Cook until the pudding thickens and some rice is visible on the surface, 10 to 12 minutes. The mixture will be fairly soupy; it will thicken as it cools.

04 Ladle into individual ramekins or dessert bowls. Serve immediately or cool and then cover and refrigerate for later use. It keeps for up to 4 days. If you wish, top with one of the optional garnishes.

3 TABLESPOONS DRIED CRANBERRIES

¼ CUP HOT WATER

**2 TO 2 ½ POUNDS TART, FIRM
APPLES, SUCH AS GRANNY
SMITHS OR STAYMANS**

⅓ CUP MAPLE SYRUP

**4 SHEETS PHYLLO (ALSO SPELLED
FILO)**

3 TO 4 TABLESPOONS WALNUT OIL

**½ CUP WALNUTS, TOASTED AND
FINELY CHOPPED**

*This impressive pastry takes very little effort to assemble and is beautiful to
behold. You create a rectangular tart without a tin by layering sheets of phyllo directly
on a parchment-lined baking sheet. Then you mound maple-glazed apple slices on
top and fold over a bit of phyllo to create a flaky frame.*

*Phyllo easy to assemble? It's true that those paper-thin sheets of dough have a
way of drying out and tearing. But even if you're phyllo-phobic (as I was until recently),
this recipe offers guaranteed success. There's no fancy folding, and a few rips won't
affect the result. Just patch them up as you go.*

*You'll find phyllo in the frozen foods case in most supermarkets. Defrost it
according to the package directions (usually overnight in the refrigerator).*

The tart is nice for brunch as well as dessert.

RUSTIC **APPLE** TART

01 Put the rack in the center of the oven and preheat to 425°F. Line a
large baking or cookie sheet (about 11 by 17 inches) with parchment paper and set aside.

02 Place the cranberries in a small bowl. Pour the water over them and
set aside.

03 Peel and core the apples. Cut them into slices about ¼ inch thick.
Scatter half of the apples in a large, nonstick skillet, and drizzle
half of the maple syrup on top. Cook over medium-high heat, tossing frequently, until the apples have softened but still hold their
shape, about 5 minutes. (The apples will release liquid as they
cook; most of it will evaporate.) With a slotted spoon, transfer the
batch to a large platter to cool. Repeat with the remaining apples
and maple syrup.

04 To assemble the tart: Wet a kitchen towel and wring it well to
remove as much water as possible. Unwrap the phyllo and set the
stack on a flat surface. Gently remove 1 sheet of phyllo from the
pile and set it on the parchment-lined baking sheet. Immediately
cover the remaining phyllo with the moist towel to prevent it from
drying out. Brush the sheet of phyllo with oil. Sprinkle with about a
third of the walnuts, leaving about a 2-inch border around the
edges. Set another sheet of phyllo on top, brush with oil, and sprinkle with walnuts. Repeat with the third sheet of phyllo. Set the
fourth sheet in place and brush with oil.

05 Mound the apples haphazardly on top of the stacked phyllo in a rectangular shape, leaving about 2 inches uncovered around the edges. Gently lift the edges of the phyllo, one side at a time, and fold them over to create a "frame" about $1\frac{1}{2}$ inches wide around the apples. (Some of the slices will end up beneath the phyllo, but most will remain exposed.) Brush the phyllo "frame" with oil. Drain the cranberries and scatter them among the apples.

06 Bake until the phyllo is golden and crisp, 9 to 16 minutes. Serve warm or at room temperature. To present the tart on a platter, transfer it with the parchment in place, and then gently pull out the parchment. To serve, slice into squares.

OTHER IDEAS

Cook the apple slices with a light dusting of cinnamon.

Make apple turnovers by following the folding instructions for preparing Phyllo Triangles (page 76).

Substitute Bosc or other firm pears for the apples. Cut them into $\frac{1}{2}$-inch slices and cook only until the edges are slightly softened, 3 or 4 minutes. Season lightly with cardamom, if you wish.

An elegant cookie that celebrates the irresistible Italian combination of pine nuts and aniseeds. It comes to you compliments of Meredith McCarty, author of an award-winning vegan dessert cookbook called Sweet and Natural.

These crescents are great dunkers and have transformed numerous skeptics into anise lovers. The dough is quickly assembled, but allow a half hour to chill it for easier handling. Actually, you can leave the dough in the freezer for days or weeks (it never hardens completely), and make the cookies when you have a yen for them. The baked crescents also freeze well.

It's most economical to purchase arrowroot flour (also referred to as arrowroot powder) from an Asian grocery or the bulk bins of a health-food store. You can also mail order it from Penzeys. The small bottles sold in supermarkets for use as a thickener are quite expensive.

When you measure the flour and arrowroot, bounce the cups gently up and down. Then add a bit more, if needed, to fill them to level capacity.

3/4 CUP WHOLE WHEAT PASTRY (NOT BREAD!) FLOUR

1/4 CUP ARROWROOT FLOUR, PLUS MORE IF NEEDED FOR SHAPING CRESCENTS

1/2 TEASPOON BAKING POWDER

1/8 TEASPOON SALT

1/4 CUP PINE NUTS

1/2 TEASPOON ANISEEDS

1/4 CUP MAPLE SYRUP

3 TABLESPOONS NEUTRAL OIL, SUCH AS CANOLA

1/2 TEASPOON VANILLA EXTRACT

PINE NUT–ANISE CRESCENTS

01 Use a sifter or set a strainer over a bowl, and measure in the flour, arrowroot, baking powder, and salt. Sift or stir to pass the ingredients into the bowl. Set aside a tablespoon of the pine nuts, and then stir the remaining pine nuts and the aniseeds into the flour mixture.

02 Pour the maple syrup into a glass measuring cup. Blend in the oil and vanilla. With a fork, stir the wet ingredients into the flour mixture until all of the dry ingredients are absorbed and the dough holds together in a mass. (The dough will be moist and sticky.) Set the dough in a small covered storage container, or wrap it in plastic. Chill in the freezer for a half hour, or until needed.

03 Set the rack in the middle of the oven and preheat the oven to 400°F. Line a baking sheet with parchment paper.

04 Slice the chilled dough in half and return half to the freezer. Scoop off about 1/2 tablespoon of dough and roll it between your palms, first into a small ball and then into a log about 3 inches long. As you set the log on the parchment, curve it into a crescent shape. (If the dough feels very sticky, lightly flour your hands with arrowroot before shaping each crescent.) Continue to create crescents from

CONTINUED

all of the remaining dough, including the portion returned to the freezer. Gently press a few of the reserved pine nuts into the top of each crescent.

05 Bake until the tops feel fairly firm, yielding only slightly to gentle pressure, and the edges touching the parchment show a hint of brown, 9 to 13 minutes. (The tops will remain pale.) Slide the parchment from the baking sheet onto a cooling rack. When the crescents have cooled, peel them off the parchment. Store in an airtight container at room temperature for up to 5 days, or freeze for up to 3 months.

OTHER IDEAS

PECAN CRESCENTS

Use $1/2$ cup toasted pecans, chopped to about the size of pine nuts, instead of the pine nuts. Increase the vanilla to 1 teaspoon and add $1/4$ teaspoon ground cinnamon instead of the aniseeds.

Are you drawn to the notion of seductively soft tapioca pearls floating in a sooth-ing ocean of Caribbean flavors? This is the kind of go-down-easy dessert that I love.

The pudding comes out either soupy or thick, depending upon the whim of tapioca, an ingredient that rarely behaves the same way twice. Despite tapioca's unpredictable nature, you can count on a gorgeous golden-orange dessert with refined taste and irresistible texture—nothing like those stodgy puddings you may remember from high school cafeteria days.

Before cooking, the little white beads known as small pearl tapioca have a diam-eter of about $1/8$ inch. After soaking overnight (a necessary step), they double in size. Look for pearl tapioca in gourmet shops, health-food stores, and Asian mar-kets, or mail order it from Zabar's. Store the uncooked pearls in a well-sealed con-tainer.

Since the size and pit-to-flesh ratio varies from one variety of mango to the next, I can't tell you how many you'll need for 2 cups of puréed flesh. Buy a bountiful num-ber, and dice any left over for garnish.

Peel the mangos with a sharp paring knife, taking care to remove as little flesh as possible. Cut the flesh away from the large central pit. If the mango is fibrous, use a knife to scrape against the pit and release as much pulp and juice as you can. If tasty mangos are hard to find, don't hesitate to use the canned purée sold in Indian grocery stores (see Other Ideas).

$1/2$ CUP SMALL PEARL TAPIOCA

ONE 13.5-OUNCE CAN UNSWEETENED COCONUT MILK (NOT THE LIGHT VARIETY)

1 $1/2$ CUPS WATER

2 TABLESPOONS RUM

$1/3$ CUP SUGAR, PLUS MORE IF NEEDED

$1/8$ TEASPOON SALT

2 CUPS PURÉED FRESH MANGO

MANGO-COCONUT TAPIOCA

01 In a bowl or storage container, cover the tapioca with an ample amount of water. Cover and refrigerate for 8 hours or overnight.

02 In a 2-quart, heavy saucepan, combine the coconut milk, water, rum, sugar, and salt, and bring to a boil. Drain and rinse the tapioca and stir it in. Cook uncovered at a gentle boil, stirring frequently to prevent the tapioca pearls from sticking to the bottom, until the mixture thickens slightly and the pearls are partially or fully translu-cent, 9 to 10 minutes.

03 Stir in the mango purée. Add more sugar if you wish, keeping in mind that the sweetness will be muted if the pudding is served chilled. Continue cooking and stirring until most of the tapioca pearls look translucent and taste tender, 1 to 8 minutes longer. The mixture will be fairly thin; it will thicken and set as it cools.

CONTINUED

(A few tips: Do not cook longer than 8 additional minutes or the tapioca may become gummy. The pearls may not become uniformly translucent, and they sometimes darken after the mango purée is added, but these factors do not affect the flavor. As long as the tapioca pearls are tender, you're okay.)

04 Ladle the pudding into 1 large or 6 individual bowls. Serve warm, at room temperature, or chilled. The texture is best when the pudding is eaten within 48 hours.

OTHER IDEAS

Stirring in a scant $\frac{1}{8}$ teaspoon of finely ground white pepper at the end of cooking adds a haunting flavor and rounds out the fruity sweetness.

In place of fresh mangoes, substitute 2 cups of canned alphonso mango purée, sold in Indian groceries. If the purée has been sweetened, reduce the added sugar according to taste. Leftover purée can be frozen for later use or blended with soymilk and frozen banana chunks to make a tropical smoothie.

3 TABLESPOONS MAPLE SYRUP

1 TABLESPOON PLUS 1 TEASPOON HAZELNUT OIL

1 ¹/₂ TEASPOONS VANILLA EXTRACT

PINCH OF SALT

4 OUNCES (¹/₂ CUP) EXTRA-FIRM OR FIRM TOFU

This sweet topping gives an elegant finish to many of the desserts in this chapter. It is thick enough to spoon out in small dollops as you would whipped cream.

For optimum taste and texture, use the fresh, refrigerated tofu sold in sealed plastic tubs (rather than the aseptic-packed variety), and purée the topping in a blender. If you're serving 4, this recipe yields 1 heaping tablespoon per serving. You can easily double or triple it.

CREAMY **HAZELNUT** TOPPING

01 Place the ingredients in a blender in the order given. Blend for 30 seconds. Scrape down the sides, and continue blending until very smooth and creamy, 30 to 60 seconds more.

02 Use immediately or refrigerate in a tightly sealed container for up to 5 days. Stir well before each use.

OTHER IDEAS

Use walnut oil instead of hazelnut oil.

MAIL-ORDER SOURCES

If you have difficulty locating high-quality ingredients locally, shopping by mail is a good option. In any case, the catalogs offered by these companies are fun to read and often quite informative. Sources for a few specialized items are provided in the pantry chapter.

GOLD MINE NATURAL FOOD CO.

800-475-3663

www.goldminenaturalfood.com

Jean Richardson is devoted to selling the best organic foods she can find, including heirloom grains and beans, sea vegetables, and traditionally made soy sauces and misos. In fact, you can come close to stocking your entire vegan pantry by ordering from her educational catalog.

PENZEYS

800-741-7787

www.penzeys.com

Nine different types of peppercorns. Four grades of cinnamon. An impressive range of high-quality spices and dried herbs, available in small or large quantities.

ZABAR'S

800-697-6301

www.zabars.com

A good source of ethnic and international gourmet ingredients, including Patak's sweet mango chutney, Merwanjee Poonjiajee & Sons Madras Curry Powder, French green lentils, niçoise olives, and imported nut oils—plus a large selection of cookware at discount prices.

ZINGERMAN'S

www.zingermans.com

888-636-8162

To learn which oils, vinegars, and condiments one knowledgeable taster considers the best in the world, consult this catalog.

INDEX

TABLE OF **EQUIVALENTS**

The exact equivalents in the following tables have been rounded for convenience.

LIQUID/DRY MEASURES

U.S.	METRIC
1/4 teaspoon	1.25 milliliters
1/2 teaspoon	2.5 milliliters
1 teaspoon	5 milliliters
1 tablespoon (3 teaspoons)	15 milliliters
1 fluid ounce (2 tablespoons)	30 milliliters
1/4 cup	60 milliliters
1/3 cup	80 milliliters
1/2 cup	120 milliliters
1 cup	240 milliliters
1 pint (2 cups)	480 milliliters
1 quart (4 cups, 32 ounces)	960 milliliters
1 gallon (4 quarts)	3.84 liters
1 ounce (by weight)	28 grams
1 pound	454 grams
2.2 pounds	1 kilogram

OVEN TEMPERATURE

FAHRENHEIT	CELSIUS	GAS
250	120	1/2
275	140	1
300	150	2
325	160	3
350	180	4
375	190	5
400	200	6
425	220	7
450	230	8
475	240	9
500	260	10

LENGTH

U.S.	METRIC
1/8 inch	3 millimeters
1/4 inch	6 millimeters
1/2 inch	12 millimeters
1 inch	2.5 centimeters